JULIAN HAWTHORNE

Incredible Mysteries: Unsolved Disappearances Vol. 2

Contents

Introduction

In the still, shadowy hours under a moon's glow, when the world pauses in hushed anticipation, a profound enigma awakens. This enigma, timeless and boundless, weaves its way through continents and cultures, etching its presence into the fabric of history. It's the enigma of unexplained vanishings, the harrowing and spine-chilling accounts of individuals who have mysteriously disappeared, leaving no trace behind.

As you venture through this book, you're embarking on an expedition into the realms of the uncharted, a deep dive into some of the most confounding and eerie disappearances known to humankind. This book transcends a mere anthology of narratives; it's a mosaic, intricately pieced together with strands of doubt, trepidation, and humanity's relentless thirst for answers.

Annually, countless individuals vanish without a hint. While many are eventually found, and some choose the path of disappearance, an alarming number remain unaccounted for, creating a void brimming with unanswered questions. What fate befell them? Where did they journey to? Were they victims of wrongdoing, overcome by natural forces, or did they step into an existence beyond our comprehension?

The incidents chronicled in this book rank among the most confounding. These accounts break the mold of logical understanding and challenge the way we perceive our reality. Each chapter immerses you in a different case of disappearance, laying bare the facts, conjectures, and persistent enigmas that shroud these mystifying vanishings.

Each narrative presents a conundrum, a maze brimming with leads and dead ends, firsthand testimonies, and contrasting hypotheses. They beckon speculation and call for meticulous investigation. These stories escort you to the fringes of the inexplicable, urging you to peer past the fabric of the ordinary world.

Yet, this book is more than an assemblage of unresolved enigmas. It is, at its core, a contemplation on the essence of disappearance. What does it signify to vanish from existence? To leave behind one's story, identity, and the life once lived? The phenomenon of disappearance taps into our deepest fears and fascinations—the dread of the unknown, the seduction of mystery, and the disturbing notion that our existence can be extinguished in a mere moment.

Delving into these pages, you'll encounter the narratives of those left in the wake—the kin and companions wrestling with the absence of their loved ones. Their stories are woven with strands of sorrow, hope, and a relentless pursuit for resolution. Their experiences remind us that the echo of a disappearance extends far beyond the individual who's gone missing, casting a lasting imprint on the lives of those left behind.

As you navigate this journey, bear in mind that these accounts are more than historical footnotes; they are living enigmas, eagerly awaiting the next piece of evidence, the breakthrough, the forthcoming chapter yet to be penned. Perhaps within these pages, you'll unearth that elusive clue, that revelation, that fragment of the puzzle that has evaded seekers for ages.

Logan Schiendelman

ogan Drew Schendelman's life story unfolds like a poignant tapestry, rich with complexities and hues of both triumph and tribulation. Born on June 27, 1996, in the verdant surroundings of Tumwater, Washington, Logan's early life was nurtured under the caring watch of his grandmother, Virginia "Jenny" Gable. Alongside his half-sister Chloe, Logan navigated the contours of a childhood marked by their mother Hannah's absence, who pursued her artistic passions at an art school in Seattle. While Hannah was not a constant physical presence, residing mostly in nearby Olympia, she remained an integral figure in Logan's life. His father, however, was a distant figure, leaving a paternal void in his upbringing.

Logan's high school years at Tumwater High School painted a picture of a young man brimming with potential and charisma. As a star athlete, particularly shining as a defensive back on the football team, Logan was a well-liked figure, known for his easygoing nature, perpetual kindness, and an infectious smile that could light up any room. His peers saw him as a popular and affable teenager, always ready to lend a hand or share a laugh.

However, beneath this veneer of popularity and athletic prowess, Logan was grappling with personal challenges. At home, he was known to be introspective and sensitive, a stark contrast to his public persona. His grandmother often reflected on Logan's struggle with his identity, particularly during his teenage years. Being of a diverse heritage—African-American, Caucasian, and Saudi Arabian—Logan faced the ugliness of racial prejudice, encountering slurs and exclusion, especially towards the end of his high school journey. These incidents left a profound impact on Logan, marking a turning point in his life.

Post-graduation in 2014, Logan's path seemed set towards Eastern Washington University, where a cohort of his high school friends planned to enroll. Yet, in an unexpected twist, Logan severed these ties, leaving his friends bewildered and concerned. He redirected his journey to Washington State University, a place where his past did not define him, and anonymity offered a fresh start. However, this decision came at a cost. Logan's social struggles at the university, coupled with academic challenges, led to a decline in his overall well-being. He eventually left Washington State University, returning to the familiarity of his grandmother's home in Tumwater.

Back home, Logan's life took another turn. His sister's boyfriend moved in, altering the family dynamics. Logan himself seemed to be in a state of flux, reportedly turning to marijuana, which may have further compounded his sense of isolation and episodes of paranoia.

In the narrative tapestry of Logan's life, his freshman year emerged as a chapter filled with personal endeavors and new connections. Earning his keep, Logan found employment in a local laundry service, engaging in various odd jobs. His work ethic extended to the pastoral setting of his great aunt and uncle's farm. On the five-acre expanse owned by Mary and Mike Ware, Logan embraced the role of a general laborer, immersing himself in the rhythms of rural life. This period of his life was not just about earning a living, but also about grounding himself in the tangible and honest work of farm life.

Amidst this backdrop of daily labor, a significant development unfolded in Logan's personal journey. He initiated contact with his African-American relatives, a side of his family previously unknown to him. This quest for familial connection was a silent venture, kept hidden from his grandmother, Jenny, out of a desire not to upset or provoke her. The eventual meeting with his mother's paternal relatives marked a poignant moment in Logan's life. For the first time, he was surrounded by family members who shared his dark skin, providing him with a sense of belonging and self-acceptance that had been elusive for so long. This experience, possibly the most affirming in recent memory, brought a newfound comfort to Logan.

However, life at home painted a starkly different picture. Tensions simmered beneath the surface, particularly due to discord with his half-sister's boyfriend. Logan's uncle poignantly noted that Logan "didn't want to be there anymore," a sentiment that underscored the domestic strife and Logan's growing discomfort in his own home. Caught in a whirlpool of emotional turmoil, unable to fully grasp his racial identity, and uncertain about his future direction, Logan found himself at a critical juncture in his life.

The morning of May 19, 2016, presented an unexpected turn in this unfolding drama. At around 7:30 a.m., Logan and Jenny, preparing for their respective workdays, crossed paths in the kitchen. This encounter sparked an unusual conversation. Jenny noticed something different about Logan that morning. He was not only up earlier than usual but also appeared anxious and unsettled. Logan confided in his grandmother about having an "epiphany" the previous night, something profound about himself that he needed to work through, though he remained vague about the details. Jenny, sensing the gravity of his revelation, suggested they discuss it further that evening after work. They parted ways that morning, each heading to their work, not realizing it would be the last time they would see each other.

The evening of Jenny's return home marked the beginning of a perplexing and distressing chapter. Upon arrival, she was greeted by an unsettling silence — Logan was nowhere to be found. Her concern escalating, she resorted to tracking his cell phone, which revealed that it had last pinged at a cell tower in Olympia, tantalizingly close to where his mother, Hannah, lived. Jenny initially thought Logan might have embarked on an impromptu visit to his mother. However, as hours turned into a day with no sign of Logan's return, her worry transformed into alarm. By May 20th, the absence of her grandson felt ominously out of character, prompting Jenny to take action. She faced a frustrating delay, however, as she couldn't report Logan missing until Monday, May 23rd, due to the closure of the police departments in Thurston and Tumwater over the weekend.

In a twist of events, Hannah herself informed the authorities that Logan hadn't visited her that day, despite his cell phone's location indicating otherwise. In fact, she had been out of touch with Logan for nearly a week, adding another layer of mystery to the situation.

The plot thickened on the afternoon of May 20th, when multiple calls flooded the police department. Concerned citizens reported a vehicle behaving erratically along the I–5 southbound lane, weaving dangerously across three lanes near mile marker 92, in the vicinity of Tumwater Maytown and the Scatter Creek rest stop, within the Rochester zip code area. Eyewitnesses reported a harrowing scene: the vehicle, seemingly driverless, eventually crashed into a concrete barrier. Some witnesses claimed to have seen a Caucasian male with red or brown hair hastily exiting the passenger side and disappearing into the dense woods nearby.

The vehicle in question, a black 1996 Chrysler Sebring convertible with the license plate AVJ8434, was discovered by the police, abandoned and parked against the concrete median barrier. When impounded, a deeper investigation revealed a trove of personal items: Logan's cell phone, wallet, ID, driver's license, debit card, $25 in cash, car keys, a bottle of water, and a bag of snacks from a nearby gas station, all found within the car. Strikingly, Logan Schindelman himself was conspicuously absent, his whereabouts shrouded in uncertainty.

This bewildering scene left more questions than answers. The discovery of Logan's personal belongings in the car, particularly his identification and essentials for travel, hinted at a sudden and unplanned departure. The mystery deepened with the eyewitness accounts of an unidentified individual fleeing the scene, further complicating the narrative of Logan's disappearance. As the search for Logan intensified, the pieces of this perplexing puzzle seemed to drift further apart, leaving his family, the authorities, and the community grappling with the haunting question: where was Logan Schindelman?

The mystery of Logan's disappearance deepened as forensic teams meticulously combed through his car for clues. They captured photographs and lifted fingerprints, hoping to piece together the events leading up to the perplexing incident. However, their efforts were hampered by cross-contamination that occurred during the vehicle's impoundment, rendering much of the evidence unprocessable. This setback in the investigation only added to the growing frustration and anxiety among Logan's family and friends.

In a parallel effort, Logan's loved ones embarked on an extensive search for the missing 19-year-old. The search operation was led by his uncle, Mike Weir, a retired Thurston County Sheriff, who brought his expertise and determination to the forefront. The woods where a Caucasian male was reportedly seen fleeing from Logan's car became the epicenter of a rigorous search. Spanning a two-mile radius, the area was scoured by teams on foot, aided by helicopters and tracker dogs. Despite their exhaustive efforts and the deployment of advanced search technologies, not a single clue pointing to Logan's whereabouts emerged.

In an effort to widen the search, posters, flyers, and billboards were erected across the county, each calling for information on Logan's disappearance. The local community was galvanized into action, with many joining the search or spreading awareness.

Meanwhile, the police turned their attention to Logan's personal space for any indications of his intentions or whereabouts. They meticulously examined his room, laptop, and phone. Their investigation revealed that Logan, having become increasingly reclusive, spent considerable time alone. He often immersed himself in movies and music and engaged in conversations with strangers online. However, there was no indication that he planned to meet any of these online acquaintances.

Intriguingly, the police uncovered that Logan had recently learned his father was residing in Saudi Arabia. This discovery led to speculation: could Logan have harbored a desire to meet his father? Adding to the intrigue, a check-in post on Facebook suggested Logan was at Olympia Regional Airport in the days following his disappearance. However, upon closer examination, investigators found the post to be a year old, a dead end in the already convoluted investigation.

Further analysis of cellular data from Logan's phone painted a picture of erratic movements. On the day following his disappearance, his phone pinged along the I-5, traveling north and south, from Olympia to Portland, Oregon. The reasons for this hour-and-a-half journey to Oregon remained shrouded in mystery. Was Logan on a reflective long drive to clear his head, or had he lost possession of his phone and vehicle to someone else?

In the wake of Logan's mystifying disappearance, a tapestry of witness accounts began to emerge, each adding a new layer of complexity to the case. These testimonies provided fragmented snapshots that further intrigued and baffled the authorities.

One particularly noteworthy account came from a female witness who approached the police with a vivid recollection. On the morning of May 20th, while commuting along the I-5, she reported seeing a young black man, believed to be Logan, in the company of two Caucasian males near the trunk of his vehicle. Her description of one of the men was striking: he was approximately six feet tall, with a notably slim build and fine, straight blonde hair cut in a bowl style. She observed that his clothes, consisting of a vest and jeans, appeared uncomfortably small for his frame. The second man, although less distinctly remembered, was described as having shoulder-length blonde hair and was clad in a flannel shirt and jeans. Due to the limited details about the second individual, authorities focused on creating a composite sketch of the first man. This sketch was released on June 30th, 2017, three days after what would have been Logan's 20th birthday, in the hope that public recognition might lead to a significant breakthrough. However, as of yet, this lead has not yielded any substantial clues. There was speculation whether one of these men could be the same individual seen fleeing from Logan's car on the interstate.

Compellingly, the same female witness noted that when she passed by the same location later that day, Logan's car was still parked there, but this time with its hood up, suggesting some mechanical issue or inspection.

Another intriguing piece of information surfaced from a different witness. This individual contacted the police to recount a sighting of a half-naked black male wandering along the interstate around the same time Logan vanished. The location of this sighting was in close proximity to known drug houses, places where Logan might have obtained marijuana. However, the identity of this half-naked individual, whether it was Logan or not, remained uncertain.

These disparate witness accounts painted a perplexing picture. They brought forth more questions than answers, fueling theories and speculations about what might have transpired on that fateful day. Each narrative offered a glimpse, a potential clue in the puzzle of Logan's disappearance, yet each also deepened the mystery, leaving authorities and loved ones grappling with the uncertainty of Logan's fate.

The enigmatic disappearance of Logan Schindelman has spawned a multitude of theories and speculations, yet concrete evidence remains elusive. While there's no direct evidence to suggest that Logan overdosed, took his own life, or met any other specific fate, the lack of clues only deepens the mystery.

Despite his known aversion to his half-sister's boyfriend, Logan wasn't known to have any enemies or individuals who might wish him harm. This aspect of his life was thoroughly examined, especially the relationship with his half-sister's boyfriend, who was brought into question regarding Logan's disappearance. The boyfriend maintained his ignorance about the entire situation and even underwent a polygraph test. While he passed the test, it's important to note that polygraph results are not infallibly accurate and should be considered with caution. Adding a layer of complexity, it was revealed that Chloe's boyfriend had a previous felony charge for assaulting a former girlfriend, a detail that could not be overlooked in the investigation.

Given that Logan was frequently using marijuana at the time of his disappearance, questions arose regarding possible drug-related motives. Could Logan have been in debt over drug transactions? Was his disappearance the result of a robbery gone awry, a hit-and-run accident, or even a case of mistaken identity? The scenarios are numerous and each as plausible as the next in the absence of definitive evidence.

Another angle considered in the case was the possibility of mental illness. Logan's internal struggles and the side effects of potential drug use could have contributed to mental health issues. His occasional paranoia, including beliefs that he was being watched through his bedroom window, suggests that a manic episode could have played a role in his disappearance.

There are those who theorize that Logan might have fallen victim to foul play. Despite extensive investigations, the county sheriff's office has found no evidence to conclusively determine Logan's fate. The haunting reality remains: there is no evidence to confirm Logan is deceased, but equally, there is no evidence to prove he is alive. This lack of definitive answers leaves a gaping void, filled with endless possibilities and theories, in the story of Logan Schindelman's disappearance. The case continues to baffle and intrigue, a puzzle that remains unsolved, keeping the hope alive that one day, the truth will come to light.

The mysterious circumstances surrounding Logan Schindelman's disappearance have raised numerous questions and theories, leaving a trail of unanswered queries. Among the most perplexing aspects is the identity of the men seen conversing with Logan near milepost 92 on the I-5. Who were they, and what was the nature of their interaction with Logan?

Another theory posits that Logan, in his quest to carve out his identity, might have chosen to abandon his old life and start afresh. While this scenario seems unlikely given the known details of his disappearance, it cannot be entirely discounted in the realm of possibilities.

The nature of Logan's "mysterious epiphany," mentioned to his grandmother on the morning of his disappearance, adds another layer of intrigue. It was highly uncharacteristic of Logan to leave home without informing anyone, fueling speculation about the nature of this revelation and its potential impact on his decision to vanish.

The mystery of what happened to Logan and where he might have gone remains unsolved. His family, refusing to give up hope, has been actively involved in efforts to locate him. They have held numerous vigils and launched a substantial internet campaign to raise awareness. The Tumwater community, rallying behind the family, helped raise a $10,000 reward for any information leading to Logan's whereabouts. Despite these efforts, Logan's disappearance remains a baffling case.

When he vanished, Logan was a 19-year-old young man of African-American, Caucasian, and Saudi Arabian descent. He stood around six feet tall, weighing between 150 and 190 pounds. He had short black hair, brown eyes, and a small scar on his left forearm. His last known attire included a black windbreaker jacket, jeans, a white shirt, and shoes, possibly of the Nike brand.

A critical health detail about Logan is his severe allergy to peanuts. Notably, when he disappeared, he did not take his EpiPen with him, a vital tool for managing potential allergic reactions.

Logan's family and friends continue to seek answers, tirelessly appealing for information across various social media platforms and news outlets. They regularly share missing person posters, hoping to spread awareness of his case far and wide. Their enduring hope is that these efforts will eventually lead to new developments, bringing them closer to understanding what happened to Logan and, ultimately, reuniting with him. The story of Logan Schindelman remains a poignant reminder of the enduring power of hope and the relentless pursuit of truth in the face of uncertainty.

The Clinton Avenue Five

Brimming with life and stories, Newark, New Jersey stands as a beacon of diversity and history in Essex County. As the most populous city in New Jersey, it's a bustling urban tapestry with over 280,000 residents spread across its 26 square miles. Just a stone's throw away from the vibrant New York City, Newark is a hub of corporate headquarters and academic institutions, including prestigious names like Rutgers, New Jersey Institute of Technology, and Seton Hall University's Law School.

The city's unique character is shaped by its five political wards – North, East, South, West, and Central. These names aren't just geographical markers; they're a part of the local vernacular, symbolizing the diverse neighborhoods and communities that make up Newark. The city's cultural tapestry is rich and varied, with an array of social statuses and lifestyles, from the urban hustle to serene suburban pockets. Newark's cultural diversity is renowned, second only to Jersey City in New Jersey.

However, the Newark of today has evolved remarkably from its tumultuous past. The 1960s were marked by racial tensions and riots, significantly altering the city's demographic and social landscape. These conflicts, fueled by unemployment, poor housing, and political strife, led to a drastic population decline and a transformed cityscape.

By the late 1970s, Newark's once-thriving population had dwindled, and the city faced a new set of challenges. Abandoned buildings became the unfortunate symbols of the city's decline, housing the homeless, squatters, and drug users. This period was not only marked by physical decay but also by the dangers it posed, leading to numerous building fires and a policy of non-intervention by fire services in vacant buildings.

Amidst this backdrop of urban decay, the mysterious disappearance of the Clinton Avenue Five in 1978 adds a layer of intrigue and sorrow to Newark's history. These five young men – Melvin Pittman, Ernest Taylor, Alvin Turner, Randy Johnson, and Michael McDowell – vanished without a trace, leaving a lingering question mark over the city's troubled past.

Clinton Avenue, where they were last seen, cuts through the heart of Newark, embodying the city's diverse residential and commercial landscape. The case of the Clinton Avenue Five, intertwined with the city's history, reflects the complexities and challenges that Newark has faced over the years.

The last confirmed sighting of Randy Johnson was around 7 p.m. on Fabian Place. Melvin Pittman, after a quick dinner and change of clothes at his Beverly Street home, vanished into the dusk, last seen near an ice cream parlor on Fabian Place. Meanwhile, Ernest Taylor, Michael McDowell, and Alvin Turner were spotted in the back of a pickup truck on Clinton Avenue, identified by a contractor familiar with the boys.

Michael McDowell's movements that night add to the puzzle. He did return home briefly, but then was seen hopping into the back of a pickup truck after 8 p.m., his mother unable to identify the driver or the other passenger.

Around 11 p.m., three of the teens were reportedly seen again near Fabian Place, but it remains unclear if all five friends reunited that night. The boys' employer, Lee Anthony Evans, claims to have dropped them off together, but this account is unverified and riddled with contradictions.

Adding to the intrigue, Rodrick Royster, then 16, alleged that he and his brother were almost part of the group that night, only to be pulled out of the truck by their father – a detail that challenges the narrative of the boys' last known movements.

The families of the missing boys, initially not alarmed, grew increasingly anxious as it became clear that no one had seen their sons since the previous night. Janet Lawson, mother of Michael McDowell, frantically searched the city, calling out for her son to no avail. The bits of information gathered were sporadic and unhelpful.

Evans, the man who claimed to have hired the boys for a moving job, stated that he had paid them and dropped them off near an ice cream parlor at 11 p.m. However, suspicions about his story arose almost immediately.

When the predominantly white police force of 1978 started their investigation into the disappearance of the five young African-American men, their initial theories ranged from the boys having run away, to being involved in a car theft gone wrong. Detective Hairston, however, doubted these theories, suggesting that evidence would have surfaced if that were the case.

Contrary to the police's initial assumptions, the families of the boys were adamant that it was out of character for their sons to disappear voluntarily. With no history of running away or legal troubles to escape from, the mystery deepened, leaving the community and the families in a state of perplexed and heartbreaking uncertainty.

The saga of the missing Newark teens, while shrouded in the unknown, captures a gripping tale of a community's relentless search for answers. These young men, known for minor mischief but far from serious troublemakers, vanished into thin air, leaving their families grappling with an endless maze of possibilities.

The case initially seemed to lack urgency, even with local media slow to catch on. The intrigue deepened when Randy Johnson's family received a chilling collect call. An anonymous male claimed the boys were held captive due to a truck heist, demanding $750 for their release. The call, traced to a payphone in Washington D.C., only added to the mystery. With no cameras in 1978 to capture the caller's identity, this lead fizzled into the unknown.

Suspicion swirled around Lee Anthony Evans, who had hired the boys for work that night. Despite passing multiple polygraph tests, Evans remained a figure of interest, his story intersecting with the boys' last known activities. Yet, without concrete evidence, the investigation hit a wall.

The case's complexity was unparalleled. Social security traces led nowhere, and limited forensic data hampered identification efforts. When the Jonestown Massacre occurred, a grim possibility emerged – had the boys been swept up in this cult tragedy? This theory, too, was debunked, leaving more questions than answers.

Despite extensive searches, interviews, and national media attention, the case remained cold. Detective Hairston described it as "the most baffling case we've ever had." As years passed, the story faded from public consciousness, but not from the hearts of those who knew the boys.

In a twist of fate, psychic Dorothy Allison stepped forward in 1986, suggesting the boys' bodies were buried near Newark Airport. Though law enforcement often viewed psychic input with skepticism, Allison's past success in aiding police investigations lent some credibility to her claims. Yet, initial examinations of the field she identified yielded no results.

It wasn't until 1996, nearly two decades later, that detectives, reinvigorated with new energy and perspective, decided to revisit Allison's theory. The case had become a legend in Newark, a haunting reminder of the unknown for the families who still sought closure.

Detectives Armando To Haney and Angel Ramos, along with Allison, mapped out ten potential excavation sites in the sprawling, overgrown field. The reason behind Allison's conviction about this location remained a mystery.

In a dramatic turn of events, psychic Dorothy Alison's haunting words about the missing Newark teens stirred a renewed sense of urgency: "I see teeth in the ground. I feel that the boys were burned after being killed... I have to go by my feelings." This chilling insight led investigators to a field nestled between Interstate 78 and Route 22, near the New Jersey Turnpike, in a desperate search for answers.

On May 14, 1996, the search operation unfolded with cadaver dogs and excavation crews focusing on Alison's ten marked sites. Despite their best efforts, the mystery only deepened as nothing was uncovered. The quest for answers led detectives back to square one, interviewing family, witnesses, and suspects, but the trail remained cold.

The case, however, refused to fade away. In 2007, a new lead emerged as Terry Lawson, sister of Michael McDowell, provided a DNA sample, hoping it might match unidentified remains found elsewhere. This reinvigorated effort saw other families follow suit, clinging to the hope of unraveling the truth behind their loved ones' disappearance.

January 2008 marked a pivotal moment. Anthony Ambrose, Chief of Detectives for Essex County, greenlit a fresh investigation. This time, the spotlight turned on Maurice "Woody" Olds, with connections to Philander Hampton and Lee Anthony Evans – the latter being the man who had hired the teens on that fateful night.

The case took a bizarre twist when Rogers Taylor, brother of missing Ernest Taylor, recounted a strange encounter with Evans. Evans, now a born-again Christian, allegedly confessed to being involved in the boys' disappearance. This confession, shrouded in ambiguity, was not enough for immediate arrest, but it cast a long shadow of doubt over Evans.

The breakthrough came from an unexpected source – Philander Hampton, Evans' cousin, then in jail, decided to confess. Overburdened by guilt, Hampton revealed a harrowing tale: Evans, enraged over a missing pound of marijuana, had orchestrated a horrifying act of retribution against the boys.

The investigators' meticulous efforts culminated in the arrest of Hampton and Evans in March 2010. Charged with murder and arson, the duo's alleged crimes painted a gruesome picture. Hampton, in a bid for a lesser sentence, became a cooperating witness, detailing the nightmarish scenario of how the boys were lured, trapped, and ultimately perished in a fire.

Despite Hampton's detailed confession and the subsequent trial, the lack of physical evidence – no human remains were ever found – posed a significant challenge. The trial, mired in the complexities of absent evidence and partially corroborated narratives, did not proceed as the authorities had hoped.

The courtroom drama surrounding the trial of Lee Anthony Evans, accused of the horrific disappearance of five young men from Newark in 1978, reads like a thriller novel, yet it's a heart-wrenching reality for the families involved. With Evans' defense team skillfully highlighting inconsistencies in key witness Philander Hampton's testimony, the case took numerous twists and turns.

Hampton, who had a checkered past marred by drug abuse and a lengthy criminal record, found his credibility under intense scrutiny. His claim that the murders happened before 9 p.m. clashed with witness accounts of seeing the teens as late as 11 p.m. This discrepancy, among others, cast a shadow of doubt over his version of events.

The prosecution's strategy was not without its flaws. In a significant misstep, they mentioned Evans' deceased brother's murder conviction, a detail deemed inadmissible by the judge. Furthermore, an attempt to incriminate Evans through a recorded phone call backfired, as his bewildered response to Hampton's accusations seemed genuine to the jury.

Evans' defense was not just a rebuttal of Hampton's claims; it raised critical questions. He questioned the logistics of how he could have corralled five young men into a closet with a single nail and without any resistance, especially given the numerical disadvantage. Moreover, Evans highlighted reports of an armed man seen with the teens and conflicting accounts of the alleged fire, sowing seeds of reasonable doubt in the jurors' minds.

After a tense deliberation process, the jury found Evans not guilty on all charges in November 2011. Juror Lenny DeLeo cited the lack of compelling evidence and Hampton's unreliable testimony as key factors influencing the verdict. The families, shattered by the verdict, lamented the absence of justice, with Michael McDowell's sister Teri Lawson poignantly stating, "Not guilty does not mean innocent."

The case of the Clinton Avenue Five is a saga of unanswered questions and unresolved grief. It's a story that has haunted Newark for decades, leaving a void in the hearts of the families who lost their sons, brothers, and cousins. They faced the unimaginable pain of not only losing their loved ones but also enduring the harrowing details of what might have happened to them.

For many, the likely scenario of the young men's fate seems clear, yet the legal system's verdict leaves room for doubt. Some believe Evans orchestrated a cunning escape from justice, while others speculate that an unidentified perpetrator is responsible. The truth behind the disappearance of Melvin Pittman, Ernest Taylor, Alvin Turner, Randy Johnson, and Michael McDowell remains buried in mystery.

Forty years later, the families of the Clinton Avenue Five are left with a legacy of sorrow, a community forever scarred by the loss, and a story that echoes the complexities of truth, justice, and the elusive nature of closure. In the absence of definitive answers, the memory of the young men endures, a poignant reminder of a mystery that continues to baffle and grieve the community.

Tionda and Diamond Bradley

In the heart of Bronzeville, a vibrant neighborhood in Chicago, Illinois, lived Tracy Bradley, a resilient single mother juggling the joys and challenges of raising four daughters in her modest apartment. Among these four spirited girls were Tionda and Diamond Bradley, each unique in their own way and the center of Tracy's world. Tionda's father remained an enigma, a mystery unsolved, adding a layer of complexity to their family story.

Tracy's life was a tapestry of strength and perseverance, managing the demands of single parenthood with unwavering determination. Despite the uncertainties surrounding Diamond's paternity, with George Washington being a figure of contention and dispute, Tracy's relationship with him was a rollercoaster of on-and-off encounters. This complicated dynamic added an additional layer of complexity to their already bustling household.

Tionda, the ten-year-old elder sister, was a beacon of honesty and outspokenness within the family circle. She possessed an innate sense of justice, coupled with an intelligence that belied her years. Yet, in the presence of strangers, she transformed into a more reserved persona, showcasing the depth and versatility of her character. Tionda's passions were as diverse as her personality – a lover of writing, bike riding, dancing, and gymnastics. She never missed an opportunity to showcase her talents in school shows, displaying a zest for life and performance.

Diamond, the three-year-old bundle of energy, was like a shadow to her older sister Tionda and their mother Tracy. Described by her sister Rita as a lively child who loved jumping from couch to couch, Diamond's boundless energy was a source of joy and laughter in their home. The bond between Tionda and Diamond was more than just sisterly; it was a bond of fierce protection and deep affection.

July 5th, 2001, marked a significant change in their routine. Rita and Victoria, the other two sisters, went to spend the night with their grandmother, leaving Tracy at home with Tionda and Diamond. That night, their home buzzed with anticipation over an upcoming camping trip planned to celebrate Victoria's birthday. Washington, too, was present that night, adding another layer to the family dynamic.

The dawn of July 6th brought with it a sense of normalcy as Tracy woke up before 6 am. She lovingly kissed her daughters goodbye, entrusting Tionda with the responsibility of watching over Diamond, a task she took seriously, always adhering to the strict instruction not to open the door to strangers. Washington accompanied Tracy that morning, dropping her off at Robert Taylor Park for her work in a summer program where she prepared lunches for children.

As Tracy and Washington left the apartment around 6:30 am, the day ahead seemed like any other. But what unfolded thereafter was a tapestry of events that would leave an indelible mark on their lives, a narrative of love, complexity, and the unfathomable depth of a family's bond.

In the bustling cityscape of Chicago, Tracy Bradley's morning at work was unfolding like any other. Employed at a summer program in Robert Taylor Park, her routine included a caring ritual: a phone call to her apartment between 7 and 8 am to check on her daughters, Tionda and Diamond. However, that particular morning, her call echoed unanswered. Tracy's heart sank with worry, yet she reassured herself, thinking perhaps her girls had succumbed to a deep, peaceful sleep.

As the clock neared noon, marking the end of her shift, Tracy's thoughts were firmly anchored on her daughters. She was picked up by Washington, and they made their way back to the apartment, a journey fraught with anxious anticipation. Upon arriving, Tracy's calls for Tionda and Diamond met only with silence. The apartment was eerily quiet, the absence of her daughters palpable. Panic surged through Tracy as she realized they were nowhere to be found. She implored Washington to assist in the search, but to her dismay, he departed, leaving her to face the growing dread alone.

In the midst of the chaos, Tracy's eyes fell upon a small pile of clothes on the couch, accompanied by a note penned by ten-year-old Tionda. The message was simple yet startling: the girls had ventured to a nearby school playground and a local store, promising a swift return. Tracy's mind raced; her daughters were well aware of the rule against leaving the apartment without her permission, let alone opening the door to strangers. This deviation from their norm sent waves of alarm through Tracy and the rest of the Bradley family.

Hours passed in a blur of frantic searching and internal turmoil for Tracy. The fear of police intervention and the potential repercussions on her family weighed heavily on her. The thought of being deemed negligent and possibly losing her other daughters was paralyzing. Yet, as the clock struck 6:30 pm, 12 hours since she last saw Tionda and Diamond, Tracy's maternal instinct overpowered her fears. She dialed 9-1-1, initially stumbling over her words, veiling the truth with a story of a nap gone wrong. But as the questioning intensified, she revealed the harrowing truth - she had left them alone to go to work.

The mystery deepened as investigators learned Tionda was enrolled in summer classes at Doolittle Elementary School but was conspicuously absent that day. Reports from neighborhood children of seeing the sisters playing outside their apartment around noon and at the school playground added layers of confusion. The authorities, though diligent, grappled with the reliability of these young witnesses, fearing a mix-up of days and times.

The investigation rapidly escalated, with a dedicated team of 100 detectives tirelessly searching through every conceivable location - from the grim depths of sewers and lagoons to the haunting emptiness of abandoned buildings and factories. The area's registered sex offenders were thoroughly questioned, and over 30 relatives faced repeated interviews. Tips flooded in by the hundreds - some bizarre, like psychics claiming knowledge of the girls' whereabouts, others chilling, suggesting horrifying fates in the clutches of ill-intent.

Among the numerous leads, one particularly unsettling theory emerged: the possibility that the girls had been abducted by a man thought to be Tionda's father, possibly whisking them overseas. Each lead, however, meandered into dead ends, leaving investigators and the family in a state of agonizing limbo.

The prevailing belief among investigators was that whoever was involved in the girls' disappearance had earned their trust, suggesting a familiar face in their lives. Faith, the girls' aunt, echoed this sentiment, firmly stating that Tionda, known for her cautious nature, would never have opened the door to a stranger. This added an unnerving dimension to the case, hinting at a betrayal of trust at its very core.

The year 2001 in Chicago was marked by an unsettling reality: in the fifteen years leading up to it, the city had witnessed only five cases of abductions by strangers. This rarity cast a shadow of doubt over the disappearance of Tionda and Diamond Bradley. Many, analyzing the statistics and piecing together the available information, found it hard to believe that the girls' vanishing act was a product of random abduction. It was a mystery that perplexed the community and baffled the authorities.

Amidst the whirlwind of investigations and interrogations, a critical piece of evidence surfaced, one that would add a new dimension to the case. Tracy Bradley, during one of her sessions with the Chicago Police, had left her phone with family members. Curiosity piqued, and with a sense of urgency, a few relatives delved into her voicemail. What they discovered was a message from Tionda, recorded on the very morning the sisters went missing. However, Tracy's cell phone, a pivotal piece in this puzzle, wasn't in her possession that morning. According to family accounts, it was with the grandmother of Tionda and Diamond.

The voicemail contained Tionda's voice, a plea laced with innocence: "Mama, this is Tionda. Mom, pick up the phone. George is at the door. Can I open the door? He said we're going to Jules to pick up the cake there. We're coming to pick you up from work." This message, seemingly mundane, held great significance - it was about a cake for their sister Victoria's birthday, planned for the following day.

The ambiguity lay in the name "George" mentioned in the voicemail. Was Tionda referring to George Washington or the family's neighbor, George Senior? This crucial detail became a focal point of speculation, as "George" was the name heard by at least ten family members who listened to the recording. Mysteriously, and for reasons unknown, this vital voicemail would later vanish, its contents no longer accessible, raising questions about whether it was deliberately deleted or simply not saved.

In a twist of fate, a few days after the disappearance, surveillance footage from the store "Jules," referenced in Tionda's voicemail, surfaced. It showed two young girls resembling Tionda and Diamond. The police, eager for any lead, asked Tracy to confirm if the girls in the video were her daughters. Initially resistant, Tracy expressed skepticism without even viewing the footage. She couldn't fathom that her daughters would be there. Nevertheless, under the weight of the situation, Tracy eventually conceded to watch the video, now in the custody of the FBI. But, in a heart-wrenching turn of events, the girls in the footage were not Tionda and Diamond. It was a mere coincidence, a false hope in an ongoing saga of despair.

Years have passed since that fateful day in 2001, and Tracy Bradley continues to hold onto hope, her prayers for her daughters' safe return echoing in the silence of unanswered questions. The search for Tionda and Diamond Bradley remains active, a poignant reminder of a mother's enduring love and the relentless quest for answers in the face of uncertainty.

In the perplexing case of the missing Bradley sisters from Chicago, one element stood out with eerie prominence: a note left on the couch, allegedly written by Tionda. This note became a crucial piece of evidence, stirring a whirlpool of speculation and intrigue. One of the girl's aunts, upon examining the note, asserted that the handwriting indeed belonged to Tionda. However, she harbored deep reservations, expressing a heartfelt belief that Tionda might have been coerced into writing it. The aunt pointed out discrepancies in the spelling and style, which seemed uncharacteristic of Tionda's usual writing, fueling doubts about the note's authenticity.

Further complicating matters, other family members questioned the very necessity of the note. They argued that if Tionda had something important to convey to her mother, she would have likely called Tracy's cell phone instead of leaving a handwritten message. This line of reasoning cast further shadows over the note's legitimacy.

The FBI, in their pursuit of clarity, compared the note with Tionda's handwriting samples provided by her school. Their analysis suggested that Tionda did indeed write the note. Yet, this revelation did little to quell the lingering questions about whether she wrote it voluntarily or under duress. These doubts continue to haunt the investigation, adding layers of mystery to an already baffling case.

George Washington, a figure central to this narrative, was interviewed by the police within the initial days of the investigation. He cooperated voluntarily, consenting to searches of his home and vehicle. During these searches, several hairs were discovered in the trunk of his Lincoln. Forensic tests revealed that these hairs could have belonged to Tionda, Diamond, or Tracy, but the ambiguity regarding their precise origin and how they ended up there left the police with limited actionable evidence.

Adding to the suspicion surrounding Washington was a receipt from Home Depot, found in his possession. The receipt detailed purchases made shortly before the girls' disappearance – gloves, garbage bags, and bleach. These items, bought simultaneously, raised eyebrows among the authorities and some members of the Bradley family. Coupled with Washington's past criminal record, which included burglary and soliciting prostitution, these findings painted a troubling picture.

Tracy Bradley's interactions with the authorities added another layer of complexity to the investigation. The police described her as uncooperative, noting her refusal to allow them to speak with her other two children, Rita and Victoria. She also declined to provide a handwriting sample for comparison with the note found on the couch. In 2002, a reported altercation occurred between Tracy and a police officer who had requested her presence at the station to discuss new leads. Tracy's spiritual advisor accused the police of violating her rights by forcibly taking her to the precinct, while the authorities maintained that she had been physically combative, necessitating restraint.

In the aftermath of her daughters' vanishing, Tracy submitted to a polygraph test, which she passed, somewhat alleviating the cloud of suspicion that hovered over her. Despite the police noting her inconsistent stories and seemingly dubious actions, Tracy was never formally named as a suspect in the case of her missing daughters.

In the years following the disappearance, Tracy's life underwent significant changes. She moved away from the area where the nightmare had unfolded and changed her phone number, perhaps in a bid to start anew while still carrying the heavy burden of her loss. Despite these changes, Tracy's commitment to finding her daughters remained steadfast. She continued to hold vigils, clinging to the unwavering belief that Tionda and Diamond were still alive somewhere out there.

The impact of the girls' disappearance reverberated through the family. Victoria, one of Tionda and Diamond's sisters, revealed that Tracy had two more children after the disappearance. These younger siblings grew up unaware of Tionda and Diamond, and it fell upon Victoria and Rita to explain the existence of their two other sisters and their mysterious fate. This revelation underscored the profound and enduring impact of the tragedy on the family.

Shalia Bradley Smith, the girls' great aunt, has been a beacon of resilience and determination in the ongoing search for Tionda and Diamond. Her pursuit for answers is fueled by a profound sense of injustice and the agonizing uncertainty that haunts the family. "We can't breathe, we can't heal; we're just in limbo," she expressed, articulating the excruciating pain of not knowing, of being unable to grieve fully without closure. Shalia, several years ago, even took the initiative to contact the family linked to Tracy's old phone number, hoping against hope that Tionda might one day call the number she once knew as her mother's.

Shalia's role in keeping the case in the public eye cannot be overstated, and her convictions regarding the case are strong. She harbors a belief that Washington might have been involved in the disappearance and suspects that the girls actually went missing a day earlier than reported, on July 5th. However, Tracy's views diverge from Shalia's; she does not believe Washington played a role in their disappearance. In a twist that complicates the family dynamics further, Tracy continued her on-and-off relationship with Washington, eventually having another child with him, a son whom Washington took into custody.

Adding to the cadre of those committed to uncovering the truth was a private detective named James Miller. Driven by a desire to help and unburdened by financial motives, he offered his services free of charge to the Bradley family. Miller's involvement brought new energy and resources to the search, as he traveled extensively in the relentless quest to find Tionda and Diamond.

The year 2007 brought a glimmer of hope in the long-standing mystery of Tionda and Diamond Bradley's disappearance, a hope that emerged from the digital realm. Shalia Bradley Smith, the tireless advocate in the search for her great nieces, received an email that would momentarily ignite a flicker of hope across the family. The email, startling in its content, contained a claim that jolted the family: "This is Tionda." Linked to this message was a MySpace page, and on it, a photograph that uncannily resembled the age-progressed images of Tionda. This discovery sent ripples of excitement and hope through the family, with even the children wondering if their long-lost relative had finally been found.

In an effort to validate this potential breakthrough, a forensic artist named Lois Gibson was brought into the fold. Gibson, renowned for her expertise, was presented with three images from the MySpace page to analyze and compare against photographs of Tionda from six years prior. Approaching the task with a blend of professional skepticism and cautious optimism, Gibson was initially searching for discrepancies, any sign that the girl in the photo was not Tionda. However, as she meticulously examined each facial feature, Gibson found herself drawing an astonishing conclusion: "Oh my God, it's her."

But this beacon of hope was soon extinguished. Further investigation into the IP addresses and other details associated with the email and MySpace page revealed no connection to Tionda Bradley. The family's soaring hopes plummeted when a man stepped forward, claiming the girl in the photograph was his daughter. DNA testing confirmed his claim, dashing the hopes that had been briefly kindled.

In 2013, another eerie development surfaced. Shalia received an email from a woman in Gary, Indiana, claiming she needed to unburden her conscience. In her message, she recounted a chilling narrative: on the morning the girls disappeared, her boyfriend was mysteriously absent. When he returned later that day, he was visibly disturbed, muttering about having done something terrible, hinting at a violent act. These harrowing details were immediately passed to the police, who initiated contact with the sender. However, for reasons unknown, the police remained reticent about this lead. Strangely, the once cooperative sender abruptly ceased communication with the authorities and withdrew from the case.

The saga took another somber turn in 2017. James Miller, the private investigator who had selflessly dedicated years to finding Tionda and Diamond, passed away following a battle with cancer. His death was a devastating blow to the Bradley family. Miller's commitment to the case was not merely professional; it was deeply personal, and the family feared that the momentum he had built might wane with his passing. They were acutely aware that replacing Miller would not be a simple matter of transferring duties; it was about finding someone who could match his dedication, passion, and intimate understanding of a case that had become a significant part of his life's work.

In the sprawling metropolis of Chicago, the mystery of Tionda and Diamond Bradley's disappearance has remained an enigma, a case that has challenged even the most seasoned veterans of the police force. One such veteran, Ed Carroll, dedicated 26 years of his career to the Chicago Police Department and was intimately involved with the Bradley case until his retirement in 2013. Reflecting on his extensive experience, Carroll shared a poignant observation about this particular investigation. He noted that in almost every violent crime case he worked on, it was possible to either implicate or absolve potential suspects. However, the Bradley case stood out as a haunting exception. It was the sole case in his entire career where he found himself unable to conclusively include or exclude anyone as a suspect, a testament to the complexity and frustration surrounding this unsolved mystery.

The year 2019 witnessed a significant development, one that stirred a mix of hope and apprehension. Shalia Bradley Smith, a steadfast beacon in the relentless search for her great nieces, took to the "Missing Diamond and Tionda Bradley" Facebook page with a heartfelt plea for the girls to return home. In a twist that seemed to be straight out of a dramatic narrative, a woman responded to Shalia's post with a simple yet profound message: "We're trying." Through a subsequent exchange of messages, the woman claimed to be Tionda, adding that she and Diamond had been together all these years. She spoke of their lives, mentioning that both had children and that Diamond was attending college. In a move that seemed to offer a glimmer of validation to her claim, the woman expressed her willingness to undergo a DNA test to prove she was indeed Tionda.

The saga of Tionda and Diamond's disappearance has not only been a journey of relentless searching but also a ritual of remembrance and hope. Each year, on the anniversary of their disappearance, the family organizes a vigil. This annual event serves as a poignant reminder of the girls, a symbol of hope, and a catalyst to reignite public interest in the case. The release of this narrative coincides with a particularly significant date: July 6, 2021. This day marks the 20th anniversary of the heart-wrenching day when Tionda and Diamond Bradley vanished.

In an effort to harness the power of community and collective memory, links have been provided in the description box for anyone who might have information related to the disappearance or current whereabouts of Tionda and Diamond Bradley. This call to action is a plea for tips or leads that could help unravel the long-standing mystery and hopefully bring closure to a family that has endured two decades of uncertainty, hope, and unyielding determination in their quest to find Tionda and Diamond.

Amy Bechtel

my Joy Roe's journey began on a sunny day in Santa Barbara, California, on August 4, 1972. Born to Dwayne and Joann Roe, she was the cherished youngest child, joining a lively household with two older sisters and an older brother. Although her story started on the West Coast, Amy's formative years were spent amidst the rugged beauty of Wyoming, in the cities of Jackson and later Douglas. It was in Douglas that her father, Dwayne, took on the influential role of city administrator, setting the stage for Amy's childhood and adolescence.

Douglas, the heart of Converse County in south-central Wyoming, is a quaint town with a population just over six thousand. It's a place where the vastness of the landscape captivates the imagination, covering less than five square miles yet rich in history and natural beauty. The Converse County School District, with its range of educational institutions from primary to high school, provided the backdrop for Amy's academic journey.

The Roe family's life in Douglas was idyllic in many ways, framed by the stunning vistas of the Medicine Bow National Forest and the Thunder Basin National Grassland. The town, steeped in a culture of horse riding and a vibrant history as a key stop on the Fremont, Elkhorn, and Missouri Valley Railroad, offered Amy a childhood filled with adventure and discovery. Whether it was exploring the wilderness, fishing, or hiking, Amy and her siblings forged a bond unbreakable by distance or time.

Amy's personality shone brightly from a young age. Described as kind, sweet, and irresistibly charming, she was the kind of person who naturally drew others towards her. Her ambition was a beacon that guided her through life, pushing her to pursue her dreams with determination and grit. Not one to shy away from speaking her mind, Amy's candidness was matched only by her careful consideration in how she expressed her thoughts.

An analytical thinker, she often observed situations closely before diving in, a trait that mirrored her approach to running. Amy's passion for running began at the tender age of 13. Initially a pastime, it morphed into a defining aspect of her high school years in Douglas, where she joined the track team. Though not a natural at first, her perseverance and dedication transformed her into a formidable runner, known for her relentless pace and unwavering positivity.

Amy's journey as a runner was a testament to her resilience. Despite starting as an underdog in her high school team, she refused to let setbacks define her. This tenacity followed her to the University of Wyoming at Laramie, where she approached cross-country coach Jim Sanchez with a determination that would eventually reshape her athletic career. Though initially struggling to keep up with her teammates, Amy's relentless spirit and sweet demeanor earned her a spot on the team and eventually a partial scholarship.

In a remarkable turnaround, Amy's junior year saw her not only secure her place on the team but also rise to prominence. By her senior year, she was setting school records and earning All-American honors, a feat that left her coach and peers in awe. Her love story with fellow athlete Steve Bechtel paralleled her athletic journey. Their shared passion for sports and the outdoors forged a deep connection that blossomed into a beautiful relationship.

After graduating in 1995, Amy's focus shifted to marathon running, with the prestigious Boston Marathon on her radar. Her performance, though not record-breaking, was a reflection of her unwavering spirit and a promise of greatness to come.

The story of Amy Joy Roe and Steve Bechtel's life together unfolds like a vibrant tapestry, rich with the colors of adventure, love, and shared dreams. Their bond, which had blossomed beautifully over time, was further solidified in marriage. Together, they embarked on a new chapter in Lander, Wyoming, a picturesque town nestled 200 miles west of Douglas. Lander, with its modest population of 12,000, was a haven for those with a zest for the great outdoors. It was here, amidst the rugged beauty of Wyoming, that their love story continued to flourish.

In Lander, they found their perfect match in the form of a cozy cottage, rented from Todd Skinner, a local rock climbing legend. This town, a hidden gem brimming with a vibrant rock climbing community, was where Steve found his calling. Amy, while occasionally joining in the climbing, remained true to her first love, running. The nearby Shoshone National Forest became her sanctuary, a place where she could lose herself in the rhythm of her strides and the beauty of nature.

As 1997 dawned, the young couple, Amy at 24 and Steve at 27, stood on the threshold of a significant milestone. After much contemplation, they decided to lay down permanent roots in Lander by purchasing their first home. This decision was more than just a financial commitment; it was a declaration of their love for the town and each other, and a step towards starting a family.

Amy and Steve juggled part-time jobs, sharing responsibilities at a local sporting goods store and Amy adding to their income with a role at a local gym. By the end of July, their dream home was a reality, and they eagerly anticipated the move.

July 24th dawned, a day marked by a shared sense of freedom and excitement. Steve, an avid rock climber, planned an adventure to Dubois, about 70 miles away, to scale a challenging rock wall with a friend. Amy, on the other hand, had a list of errands to run, a prelude to her cherished running routine.

Steve, aware of Amy's passion for running, didn't think much of it when she didn't mention her plans to run that day. To him, it was as routine as brushing teeth. He left for his climbing adventure, unaware of the sequence of events that would unfold in his absence.

Amy's day was a whirlwind of activity. She started at the Wind River Fitness Center, where she co-taught a children's weight training class. Recently certified as a trainer, Amy was building a foundation for a future dream she shared with Steve – opening their own gym. Her colleagues at the gym found her to be a delightful presence, although she remained somewhat of a mystery, never fully opening up about her personal life.

After leaving the gym at noon, Amy's day continued with a flurry of tasks, including visits to the recycling center and calls to utility companies for their new home. Her last known errand was a brief stop at a local photo store, Camera Connection, where she discussed entering a photo contest. This would be the last confirmed sighting of Amy that day.

Amy's next destination was Sinks Canyon Campground in Shoshone National Park, where she planned to map out a 10K race course. Changing into her running attire – a yellow tank top, black shorts, and Adidas shoes – she drove her white Toyota Tercel into the heart of the park. Known for her resilience in overcoming physical challenges like shin splints, Amy was determined to complete her run. She left her car unlocked at the Burnt Gulch cutoff, with the keys hidden under papers on the passenger seat.

The exact time of Amy's departure on her run remains a mystery, pieced together from unconfirmed sightings. Her car, left at the spot she parked, became a silent witness to her absence. Meanwhile, Steve's day took an unexpected turn as threatening weather conditions at the rock wall in Dubois forced him and his friend to abandon their climbing plans. Unbeknownst to them, this decision would lead to a chain of events that would change their lives forever.

As Steve drove back to Lander in his blue pickup truck, unaware of the eerie stillness that had settled over Amy's last known location, the story of their day – a tapestry of love, dreams, and unspoken goodbyes – hung in the balance.

Steve Bechtel's return to their empty home around 4:00 to 4:30 p.m. was met with an unsurprising calm. It was common for Amy to immerse herself in her late afternoon runs, leaving Steve to his own devices. He busied himself with household chores, relishing the solitary quiet of their shared space. A brief visit to their neighbor, Todd Skinner, added a social interlude to his evening, followed by an attempt to connect with a philosophical friend, leaving a message at 4:43 p.m., as later confirmed by the call log.

As the afternoon sun dipped towards the horizon, Steve's initial ease began to unravel into threads of worry. Amy's absence stretched beyond the usual bounds of her running routine. Each passing minute seemed to weigh heavier on Steve's mind, stirring a growing sense of unease.

Around 6:45 p.m., a knock on the door momentarily broke the spell of Steve's anxious wait. It was Todd Skinner and his girlfriend, ready for a movie night, inviting Steve to join. It was then that Steve voiced his concerns about Amy's prolonged absence. Opting to stay behind, he busied himself with tasks, a vain attempt to distract from the worry gnawing at him. A trip to their newly purchased house, a stop at the sporting goods store they both worked at, and then back home - the evening passed with no sign of Amy.

By 9 p.m., Steve's thoughts spiraled towards the possibility of Amy visiting her parents, a plan previously put on hold due to a family tragedy. A call to Amy's mother, Joanne, only deepened the mystery; Amy hadn't been seen there either. Steve's concern morphed into action as he embarked on a quest to find her, driving to her usual running spots, but each location echoed back with her absence. A nagging thought about missing a potential call for help turned his vehicle back home, leaving Sinks Canyon unchecked - where, unbeknownst to him, Amy's car remained parked.

In a flurry of phone calls, Steve reached out to Amy's family and his own, the concern in his voice painting a stark picture of the situation. By 10:30 p.m., with no trace of Amy and the night deepening, Steve dialed 911, his tone perplexingly casual as he reported her missing.

The arrival of a sheriff's deputy at their home around 10:45 p.m. coincided with Todd and his girlfriend's return from the movies. As they joined the conversation, the potential of Amy being injured while running in Sinks Canyon emerged. Todd and his girlfriend volunteered to check the area, leaving Steve with the deputy.

Their discovery of Amy's unlocked car at the Burnt Gulch turnoff, keys hidden under her to-do list, intensified the mystery. Despite their search around the car, no clues emerged, and their calls into the darkness went unanswered. A call to Steve around 1 a.m. from Skinner's girlfriend set in motion the involvement of the Fremont County Search and Rescue, led by Chip Williams.

Steve, accompanied by a friend, arrived at the scene with supplies, ready to search through the night. Williams, however, decided to wait for daylight, given the complexity of the terrain. A small team of skilled climbers from Lander, friends of Amy and Steve, began an immediate search, while a larger group assembled for a thorough effort at dawn.

By 5:00 a.m., the search party had grown, yet Amy remained elusive. The expertise of the searchers, accustomed to the challenges of Lander's wilderness, found no trace of Amy. Williams, puzzled by the absence of any evidence, began to contemplate the worst.

As hours turned into days, the search for Amy evolved from a rescue mission to a complex investigation. The lack of clues, the unremarkable state of her car, and the absence of any signs of a struggle or animal attack deepened the mystery. Amy's brother Nels, arriving on the scene, quickly sensed the gravity of the situation, suspecting foul play.

The search team, with its intimate knowledge of the local geography, scoured the area thoroughly. The Fremont County Sheriff's Department, revisiting Amy's car, found nothing but her to-do list, with notes on the planned 10K. Dave King, formerly of the department, summed up the baffling nature of the case: a complete lack of evidence, a scenario that defied all typical outcomes of a lost or injured person in the wilderness.

As dawn broke on the second day of the search for Amy, the community's response was nothing short of extraordinary. The once tranquil expanse of Sinks Canyon and its surrounding areas transformed into a bustling hub of activity, as hundreds of volunteers converged to join the effort. The search area expanded relentlessly, eventually covering a staggering 20 square miles. Volunteers, some on horseback and others on ATVs, combed the landscape meticulously, while tracking dogs, with their keen noses, scoured the terrain. Even a helicopter, equipped with an infrared heat-seeking sensor, soared above, scanning for any sign of Amy.

A makeshift command post, resembling a small village of tents and equipment, sprung up near Fry Lake, orchestrating the extensive search operations. For five relentless days, searchers worked tirelessly in rotating 12-hour shifts. They traversed rugged canyons, scaled hills, and covered vast tracts of wilderness, marking each area they had searched. Yet, despite their exhaustive efforts, Amy remained elusive.

On the fourth day, a flicker of hope ignited when footprints, seemingly matching Amy's shoes, were found. But this hope was quickly extinguished when a local boy admitted to camping in the area with the same shoes. No evidence was found – not a piece of clothing, not a drop of blood, nothing to suggest Amy had even been there.

Five days into the search, on July 29th, the nature of the case shifted dramatically. The Fremont County Sheriff's Department reclassified Amy's disappearance from a missing-persons case to a criminal investigation, with Dave King, a figure of some controversy, at the helm. For Chip Williams, leading the search efforts, the decision to call off the search was heart-wrenching. He later reflected on the profound disappointment and helplessness felt by all involved, realizing that despite their skill and dedication, they were no closer to finding Amy than when they started.

The investigation ramped up as sheriff's deputies canvassed Lander, setting up roadblocks, questioning residents, and spreading awareness. Amy's family, consumed by grief and determination, blanketed the town with flyers and yellow ribbons. The case captured media attention, flooding authorities with over a thousand tips daily, yet none led to a breakthrough.

On July 30th, the FBI was called in to assist, with 25 agents from the Casper and Denver field offices joining the investigation. For Amy's mother, Joanne, the surreal nature of the situation was overwhelming, describing it as an out-of-body experience that defied comprehension unless personally endured.

During this time, a potential lead emerged from Jim and Wendy Gibson, owners of the Landers Pronghorn Motel. They reported seeing a blonde woman running along Loop Road, in a manner reminiscent of Amy's running style, and later, a glimpse of something or someone in the backseat of Amy's car. This sighting fueled speculation and what-ifs, but yielded no concrete answers.

Investigators began to consider the possibility that Amy's disappearance might be linked to someone she knew. As is often the case, scrutiny fell on Amy's husband, Steve Bechtel. On August 5th, Steve faced intense questioning from Dave King and FBI agent Rick McCullough. The conversation took a turn when McCullough, presenting a folder, accused Steve of involvement in Amy's disappearance and pressed for a polygraph test. Although Steve initially agreed, he later declined on his lawyer's advice.

The following day, authorities executed search warrants on Steve and Amy's cottage and his truck. This was partly motivated by a new witness claim of seeing Steve's blue pickup on Loop Road the day Amy vanished, with a blonde woman in the passenger seat. The search yielded little, but investigators seized journals belonging to both Amy and Steve, which hinted at possible marital discord.

As the journals were scrutinized by Amy's family, some voiced suspicions about Steve's behavior, suggesting he may have been controlling or even abusive. This cast a shadow over Steve's refusal to take the polygraph and widened the rift between him, law enforcement, and Amy's family. Steve's participation in The Today Show, where he expressed frustration at being portrayed as the villain, did little to quell the growing public speculation.

Amidst the division, Amy's family and Steve pursued separate efforts to find her. Steve organized volunteers to distribute flyers nationwide and established a reward fund, raising it to $50,000 in hopes of enticing information.

By the end of August, the Fremont County Sheriff's Department publicly acknowledged their investigation was hitting a dead end. The search for Amy had mobilized a community, captivated the nation, and now, it was mired in uncertainty and suspicion, with more questions than answers.

In the unfolding mystery of Amy's disappearance, an unexpected turn arose when NASA informed investigators that the Russian space station Mir had been orbiting over the area at the time Amy went missing. This revelation brought a glimmer of hope, as there was a possibility that satellite photography from Mir could provide vital clues. Eagerly, investigators submitted a request for these images.

Amidst the ongoing search, the 10K race that Amy had passionately planned came to fruition on September 28th. The event was rechristened as the Amy Bechtel Hill Climb, transforming into a poignant tribute and a fundraiser for future search efforts. Over 150 locals, along with Amy's family members, participated, tracing the course Amy had laid out. However, the race was overshadowed by an undercurrent of tension between Amy's family and Steve, culminating in Steve severing all communication with the family after the event.

Steve vowed to persist in the search for Amy, stating his willingness to offer rewards and continue the search alone. His words echoed the torment of uncertainty, reflecting on the unbearable scenarios that haunted his thoughts - whether he would ever see Amy again, and if so, in what condition.

Tips about Amy's possible sightings poured in from across the country - Texas, Wisconsin, New Mexico, Utah, Colorado, and Florida - but each led to a dead end. As 1997 drew to a close, both Amy's family and Steve were left grappling with the unknowns of her fate.

In early 1998, the eagerly awaited images from the Mir Space Station arrived, only to bring disappointment as cloud cover obscured any useful detail. The case gained national attention, with Amy's family appearing on the Geraldo Rivera Show in February and People magazine featuring her story in March. Despite these efforts, leads, like one from Sarasota, Florida, where Amy was reportedly seen confused in a parking lot, ultimately led nowhere.

In June, authorities reignited the search with new vigor, bringing in scuba divers to search Fry Lake, but to no avail. Meanwhile, significant developments occurred on various fronts: Sheriff Dave King resigned after being charged with a crime, Amy's father passed away without knowing her fate, and Steve tried to move forward with his life, still haunted by her disappearance.

Six years after Amy vanished, in April 2003, a new suspect emerged - Dale

Wayne Eaton, convicted for the 1988 murder of Lisa Marie Kimmell. Eaton's criminal history and proximity to the area where Amy disappeared made him a person of interest. Despite this, Eaton refused to cooperate with law enforcement, leaving the investigation at a standstill.

Steve, while acknowledging Eaton's heinous crimes, remained skeptical of his involvement in Amy's case, perceiving the focus on Eaton as a convenient answer to a complex question. In 2004, nearly seven years after Amy's disappearance, Steve had her declared legally dead and later remarried, starting a new chapter in his life while continuing to live in Lander.

Amy's family, seeking a meaningful way to honor her memory, transformed the reward money into athletic scholarships in her name at the University of Wyoming and Northwest College.

In 2011, the Fremont County Sheriff's Department revisited the case with Detective John Zerga leading a fresh investigation. Zerga's review highlighted numerous flaws in the initial investigation, including tunnel vision around Steve as a suspect and mishandling of evidence. Over the years, various leads, including a watch similar to Amy's and a pen possibly belonging to her, were investigated, but no conclusive evidence was found.

The years since Amy's disappearance have been marked by sporadic efforts, hopeful leads, and continued heartache for her family. The lack of closure and the haunting possibility that the truth may never be uncovered remains a heavy burden. The case of Amy's disappearance, shrouded in mystery and marred by investigative missteps, continues to echo through the lives of those touched by her story.

Rachel Louise Cook

Rachel Louise Cook's journey began on a sunny May 10th in 1982, in the heart of Georgetown, Texas. Born to Robert and Janet Cook, she was the first sparkle in their eyes, soon to be followed by her sister Joanne. The Cook family nestled their lives in a ranch-style home in the North Lake subdivision, a charming area about 30 miles north of the vibrant city of Austin. Their home, like many in the area, sat on a generous plot of land, offering a serene and spacious living environment.

Georgetown, the county seat of Williamson County, is renowned for being home to the prestigious Southwestern University, the oldest university in Texas. Spanning 24.9 square miles at the time of Rachel's childhood (later expanding to 54.3 square miles), the city exuded a quaint small-town ambiance that was both welcoming and tightly-knit. It was a place where neighbors knew each other by name, and the sense of community was palpable. The Cook family relished this atmosphere, finding comfort in the safety and familiarity of their surroundings.

In this nurturing environment, Rachel's personality blossomed. Her father, a software engineer, instilled in her a logical and structured approach to life, while her mother, a beloved teacher at the local Georgetown High School, nurtured her creative and emotional side. This fusion of influences was instrumental in shaping Rachel into a well-rounded individual, brimming with intelligence, creativity, and ambition.

From a tender age, Rachel's aspirations were clear. She wasn't just a dreamer but also an achiever, always open about her goals and ambitions. Her active lifestyle, fostered by the vast rural landscapes of Georgetown, was a testament to her energy and vivacity. She spent countless hours outdoors, exploring, playing, and soaking in the beauty of nature, often until the sun dipped below the horizon.

Rachel's infectious personality, a blend of cheer, kindness, and humor, left a lasting impression on everyone she met. Friends and family recall her ability to light up a room with her presence and her knack for making people laugh. Shannon Leach, a lifelong friend, fondly remembers Rachel's magnetic charm: "Rachel was one of those people you loved to be around. She was funny, beautiful, and just a good person."

But Rachel was not just a fun-loving outdoor enthusiast. She had a flair for fashion, often creating stunning outfits that turned heads and set trends among her peers. Shannon reminisced, "She could create these outfits that nobody else could get away with, and they always looked amazing on her."

As Rachel grew, so did her athletic abilities. She discovered a passion for running, a skill she honed with dedication and determination. Her father noted that running was an intrinsic part of her, a way for her to connect with herself and her surroundings. During her high school years, Rachel became a standout in long-distance track and cross-country, often embarking on morning runs that spanned several miles around her neighborhood.

However, beneath the surface of this idyllic life, a shadow loomed. Rachel's passion for running, a source of joy and freedom, would later intertwine with the mystery of her sudden and heart-wrenching disappearance. As she approached the end of her high school career, Rachel's beauty and charismatic personality attracted many admirers. She had a few relationships, including one that ended in a difficult breakup, which later became a topic of much speculation.

At 18, Rachel made an unexpected decision to enter the Miss Georgetown competition. Despite not winning, her mother recalls that Rachel cherished the experience. It was around this time that Rachel set her sights on a future in fashion, planning to move far from home to San Diego, California. Her parents harbored concerns about her safety in such a vast and unfamiliar city, but they supported her dreams nonetheless.

In San Diego, Rachel's life took a new turn. She met Greg, a fellow student, and the two quickly fell in love. Their relationship was one of mutual respect and admiration, and Rachel's parents were impressed by Greg's dedication to their daughter. The couple's plans for a future together were full of promise and excitement.

Sadly, this bright future was never to be. During a holiday visit home in 2001, Rachel's life took a tragic and mysterious turn. She enjoyed her time with family and Greg but decided to extend her stay for a cousin's wedding. This decision led to an afternoon shopping trip with her father, a seemingly ordinary event that would precede one of the most baffling and heartbreaking mysteries in Georgetown's history.

As the new year dawned, Gregg returned to California, leaving Rachel in Texas with a promise to keep in touch. Their excitement for the future was palpable, as they eagerly anticipated building a life together. Meanwhile, Rachel, surrounded by the familiarity of her family home, reached out to her best friend Shannon, planning to meet on the evening of January 10th, the same day she was scheduled to go shopping with her father.

However, two days prior to their planned outing, on January 8th, Rachel found herself in an unsettling situation. She attended a local party where many of her high school friends gathered. The evening took a distressing turn when her ex-boyfriend, who was also present, began to harass her. Witnesses at the party noted that he had been drinking and, despite starting the conversation casually, he increasingly expressed his desire to reunite with Rachel. Firm yet kind, Rachel made it clear that she had moved on and was seeing someone new. This confrontation, with its underlying tension and the ex-boyfriend's ominous remark of not wanting to live without Rachel, would later become a focal point in the mystery of her disappearance.

January 10th started as an ordinary day in the Cook household. Rachel's parents and sister, Joanne, went about their morning routine while Rachel slept on the couch. As they left for the day, they bid her a sleepy goodbye. Later, Rachel spoke with Gregg over the phone around 9:00 a.m., sharing her plan to go for her usual morning jog. This conversation would be the last confirmed communication with Rachel.

Dressed in her running attire—a green sports bra, gray shorts, white shoes (either Adidas or Asics), and carrying her bright yellow Sony Walkman—Rachel set out for her run, unknowingly for the last time. The precise time of her departure remains unknown, but it's believed she never returned home.

When Robert, her father, returned home around 3:00 p.m., he was surprised to find the house empty, especially given their shopping plans. Noticing Rachel's purse and cell phone left behind, an unusual occurrence for her, he grew concerned. He reached out to Shannon, only to learn that she hadn't seen Rachel either. Shannon later recounted her worry upon learning that Rachel had left without her personal belongings, which was out of character for her.

Janet, Rachel's mother, initially thought Rachel might be working at the local restaurant, Wildfire. However, after confirming that Rachel was not scheduled to work, the family's concern escalated. The next morning, with Rachel still missing, a chilling reality dawned upon them. A phone call to the restaurant revealed a mix-up; it was a different Rachel who had worked the previous night, not their daughter.

The Cook family sprang into action, searching for any clue to Rachel's whereabouts. They realized the only items missing were her running clothes. In a desperate bid to find her, Robert drove along her jogging route, while Janet checked the local hospital, but their efforts were in vain.

Their next step was to file a missing person's report with the Williamson County Sheriff's Department. However, they felt their concerns were not taken seriously, with suggestions that Rachel might have gone to Mexico with her boyfriend. Undeterred, the Cooks organized a large search party to scour the area along Rachel's jogging path.

When the Sheriff's Department finally became involved, they halted the search party, fearing that evidence might be compromised. The department then began interviewing neighbors to establish a timeline. Remarkably, several neighbors had seen Rachel jogging that day, offering crucial sightings that narrowed down the time of her disappearance.

The last confirmed sighting of Rachel Cook on the day of her disappearance was particularly poignant, as it came from a couple who were not just residents of the same area but also acquaintances of the Cook family. Situated just a few hundred yards from the Cook residence, this couple recalled a moment that now holds significant weight in the ongoing mystery. As they were reversing out of their driveway, Rachel jogged past the back of their vehicle. Continuing onto the street, they noted Rachel heading in the direction of her home. It was approximately 10:45 a.m., and Rachel was tantalizingly close to safety, less than 200 yards from her family's doorstep.

However, beyond this sighting, Rachel seemed to have vanished into thin air. Adding to the complexity of the case were reports from the day of her disappearance, suggesting the presence of unfamiliar people and vehicles in the North Lake subdivision. This was unusual for this community, where residents typically recognized each other's vehicles. But on that fateful day, multiple witnesses reported seeing unfamiliar cars, including a late-model white Camaro or Trans Am. Others mentioned a similar vehicle, but in blue.

These sightings sparked intense interest, especially as Sheriff's Detective Larry Hawkins revealed the volume of reports concerning the white Camaro.

More disturbingly, one witness described a male with dark slicked-back hair in the white Camaro, talking to a jogger. While it wasn't confirmed if this jogger was Rachel, the correlation was alarming. Adding to the unease was the account of a female seen struggling in the back seat of a vehicle, although her identity could not be confirmed as Rachel.

In addition to the Camaro, a white pickup truck was also seen in the subdivision, acting suspiciously. This truck was reported to have slowed down next to a female jogger, seemingly attempting to engage with her. While this jogger's identity was not confirmed, given the small number of women jogging in the area that morning, it was believed to be a strong possibility that it was Rachel.

In response to these disturbing reports, the Sheriff's Department made two critical decisions. Firstly, they initiated record searches for vehicles matching the descriptions given, hoping to identify who was in the neighborhood that morning. Secondly, they requested assistance from the Texas Rangers, indicating the severity of the situation.

The following day, a massive search was organized, involving multiple law enforcement agencies, ATVs, horses, helicopters, tracking dogs, Equusearch, and local volunteers. Despite this extensive effort, no trace of Rachel was found. Detective Hawkins later expressed his frustration, highlighting the complete absence of any evidence pointing to a crime scene.

The official search was eventually called off, but volunteers and Equusearch members continued their efforts, expanding their search radius each time. Unfortunately, none of the items found and turned in led to any significant leads.

As the case garnered media attention, thousands of tips poured into the

Sheriff's Department. Investigators conducted hundreds of interviews, including with Rachel's ex-boyfriend, who was an early suspect. However, no evidence linked him to Rachel's disappearance. Rachel's sister, Joanne, expressed her suspicions about the ex-boyfriend, recalling an incident where he showed up at their home drunk and belligerent.

Authorities also examined multiple vehicles matching the descriptions of the Camaro, Trans Am, and white truck, but again, no evidence was found linking them to Rachel. A tip from a local high school student about being in the area that morning ultimately led nowhere after thorough investigation.

The case took another turn as searchers considered the possibility of Lake Georgetown, located several miles from the Cook home. With a depth of 85 feet and covering 1,297 acres, the lake presented a daunting new avenue of investigation.

The relentless quest to uncover the truth about Rachel Cook's disappearance led investigators to deploy dive teams into Lake Georgetown repeatedly. During these expeditions, several submerged vehicles were discovered, but upon examination, it was determined that these vehicles, all stolen, had no connection to Rachel's case. Despite numerous searches over the years, the murky depths of Lake Georgetown remained silent about Rachel's fate.

To aid in the investigation, composite drawings were created based on eyewitness accounts of individuals seen in the neighborhood on the day Rachel vanished. These images were widely circulated through media outlets, yet no substantial leads materialized from them. With the trail growing colder, investigators revisited the basics, scrutinizing Rachel's family and her boyfriend, Greg, who had returned to partake in the search efforts. Greg faced thorough questioning about his relationship with Rachel and any potential issues she might have had with others. His alibi, confirmed by phone records, eventually cleared him of suspicion.

Rachel's parents, Robert and Janet, also underwent polygraph tests. Janet passed without issue, but Robert's results were inconclusive on one critical question—whether he knew Rachel's whereabouts. He later explained his belief that Rachel was in heaven, which might have influenced his response. Despite this, the investigation found no evidence implicating the family, and the case tragically began to fade into obscurity.

Years passed, and in 2004, a renewed effort to solve Rachel's case was initiated by a newly elected sheriff. A task force comprising sheriff's detectives, Texas Rangers, the Austin Police Department's Cold Case Unit, and the FBI was formed to reexamine every detail of the case. Despite their exhaustive efforts, the task force was unable to unearth any new leads, leaving Rachel's case shrouded in mystery.

In 2006, a startling development emerged when convicted killer Michael Keith Moore confessed to abducting and murdering Rachel. Moore, serving life sentences for other crimes, claimed responsibility for Rachel's disappearance, describing a horrific sequence of events that culminated in him disposing of her body in Matagorda Bay. Detectives Hawkins and Lindemann interviewed Moore in prison, and he agreed to assist in locating Rachel's remains as part of a plea deal.

Divers scoured the area of Matagorda Bay specified by Moore but found nothing. Moore's story was lent credence by the fact that he had been driving a white pickup truck similar to the one seen in the area on the day of Rachel's disappearance. However, in a shocking courtroom twist, Moore recanted his confession, claiming he had fabricated the story for personal gain. This revelation left the Cook family and investigators devastated and angry, thrusting the case back into uncertainty.

Persistent tips about a large piece of property where Rachel might be buried led to several searches, utilizing ground-penetrating radar, but these efforts yielded no results. The emotional toll of Rachel's disappearance was immense, leading to the breakdown of Robert and Janet's marriage. Robert Cook became a tireless advocate for missing persons, dedicating his life to the search for Rachel and helping others in similar situations. Tragically, Robert passed away in 2014 without finding the answers he so desperately sought.

Further searches were conducted in 2017 and 2018, including a dig near Liberty Hill and the recovery of a white Pontiac Trans Am in Dallas. Cadaver dogs indicated the presence of human remains, yet nothing was found. The forensic examination of the Trans Am revealed bloodstains, but the investigation's details remain confidential to maintain its integrity.

To this day, the mystery of Rachel Cook's disappearance remains unsolved, a haunting reminder of the fragility of life and the enduring pain of the unknown. The Cook family's relentless pursuit of the truth, despite heartbreak and setbacks, stands as a testament to their love and unwavering commitment to finding Rachel.

Angela Hammond

On a crisp February day in 1971, in the bustling city of Kansas City, Kansas, a bundle of joy named Angela Marie Hammond was welcomed into the world by her ecstatic parents, Marsha and Christopher Hammond. Angela, affectionately called Angie by her doting family, marked the beginning of their journey into parenthood, filling their lives with immense happiness and love.

From her earliest days, Angie radiated a contagious energy that charmed everyone around her. The Hammond family, embracing the whirlwind of parenthood, faced the universal challenges of balancing work, finances, and family life. In 1975, with Angie at the tender age of four, the family embarked on a new adventure, relocating to the quaint town of Clinton, Missouri, about 80 miles from the hustle of Kansas City. This move was partly influenced by the proximity to Marsha's parents, offering a supportive environment for young Angie.

Clinton, a charming town nestled in Henry County, boasted a close-knit community of around seven to eight thousand residents. This idyllic setting, with its sprawling landscapes, serene Truman Lake, and the soon-to-be-opened Katy Trail State Park, offered a perfect backdrop for a young Angie to explore and grow.

The transition from city life to the small-town charm of Clinton brought a fresh perspective to the Hammond family. Angie, a dynamic and spirited child, immediately fell in love with her new surroundings. Her infectious energy and joyful disposition endeared her to everyone she met.

As the Hammond family settled into their new life, they welcomed another child, a younger brother for Angie. Despite the inevitable challenges, Chris and Marsha worked tirelessly to provide a nurturing environment for their children. However, over time, it became apparent that their marriage was facing difficulties. They amicably separated, ensuring that Angie and her brother continued to receive all the love and care they deserved.

Following the separation, Chris moved back to Kansas, settling in Oly, 80 miles away, yet remained an integral part of his children's lives. Marsha moved to a secluded farm in Montrose, 20 miles from Clinton, but for Angie, Clinton always felt like home.

Angie blossomed into a fun-loving, free-spirited young woman, renowned for her vibrant personality and infectious energy. Her father, Chris, fondly described her as a "fun-loving girl who loved to be around people." Her charisma and warmth drew people to her, making her a popular figure in her community.

As Angie grew older, she yearned for a partner to share her life's journey. In 1990, at the age of 19, she met Rob Schaeffer, an 18-year-old high school star athlete with dreams of serving in the military. Their connection was instant and profound, leading to a whirlwind romance. They quickly became inseparable, dreaming of a future filled with possibilities and mutual support.

Their relationship took a significant turn in January 1991 when Angie announced her pregnancy. Rob, supportive and excited, proposed to Angie, and the young couple eagerly embarked on their new life together, despite financial challenges. They found a modest mobile home and began preparing for their baby's arrival.

However, their dreams and aspirations were tragically interrupted on the night of April 4, 1991. Angie and Rob had spent a pleasant evening at a family barbecue at Marsha's home. Later that night, Angie, feeling tired, decided to call it an early night and headed home, planning to use a payphone to inform Rob. She stopped at a phone booth near the Food Barn supermarket, just blocks away from Rob's parents' home.

As they chatted on the phone, Angie and Rob shared the day's stories and their plans for the weekend, unaware that this conversation would be their last. The events that unfolded next would leave an indelible mark on the town of Clinton, turning Angie's story into a haunting mystery that lingers to this day.

The conversation between Angie and Rob took an ominous turn when Angie mentioned a mysterious truck that had been circling the area, its presence sending a shiver of unease down their spines. Rob listened intently as Angie described the eerie behavior of the vehicle, a green Ford pickup from the late '60s or early '70s, which had vanished only to reappear again, parking ominously close to her car by the phone booths.

Angie, with a whisper of apprehension in her voice, relayed to Rob the actions of a man who emerged from the truck and entered the adjacent phone booth. Rob, trying to remain calm, suggested that perhaps the man was just lost and needed directions. However, the situation escalated quickly when the man, after a brief moment in the booth, returned to his truck and began searching for something with a flashlight. Angie's fear was palpable as she described the man to Rob – a Caucasian male, scruffy with a beard and mustache, dressed in overalls, a dark baseball hat, and black-rimmed glasses. The words 'filthy' and 'bearded' resonated in Rob's mind.

In a moment that seemed to stretch into eternity, Angie, with her characteristic boldness, asked the man if he needed the phone. His denial added to the tension. Shortly after, Rob heard Angie's terrified scream over the phone, followed by a chilling male voice. Dropping the phone in a panic, Rob raced towards Angie, his heart pounding with fear and urgency.

As he drove, a truck sped past him in the opposite direction. It was then that he saw a woman in the front seat, fighting with the driver. Rob's heart sank as he recognized Angie, her voice piercing through the partially rolled-down window. In a desperate attempt to save her, Rob executed a hasty U-turn, but fate was cruel. His truck, damaged in the frantic maneuver, failed him, grinding to a halt as the abductor's truck disappeared into the night.

This marked the last sighting of Angela Hammond. Rob, in a state of despair, attempted to chase the truck on foot but to no avail. Another vehicle approached, and Rob, filled with desperation, pleaded for help to get to the police station. There, he recounted the harrowing tale, providing a detailed description of the abductor and his vehicle – a distinctive two-tone Ford truck with a unique fish decal on the back window.

Despite the vivid description and a composite sketch, the investigation hit dead ends and swirling rumors. Rob faced scrutiny, with suspicions cast upon him due to the dramatic nature of his story. However, his consistent recounting of events and evident distress gradually cleared him of doubt.

As the investigation expanded with FBI involvement, another name surfaced – Bill Barker, Angie's ex-boyfriend. Rumors swirled about the paternity of Angie's unborn child, adding complexity to an already baffling case. Both Barker and Rob underwent intense questioning, with Barker adamantly denying any involvement or motive.

The days following Angie's disappearance were fraught with tension and unanswered questions. The small-town community of Clinton was rocked by the incident, with everyone grappling for answers. Angie's fate remained shrouded in mystery, leaving a haunting void in the hearts of those who knew and loved her.

The mystery of Angela Hammond's disappearance took a dramatic turn as Rob actively joined the search efforts, his sincerity and distress evident to all. Despite feeling targeted by investigators, Rob and Bill Barker, Angie's ex-boyfriend, cooperated fully, both passing polygraph tests, which shifted the focus away from them. Detective Parsons clarified their involvement as primary witnesses, not suspects, further bolstered by local sightings of the suspicious truck on the night Angie vanished. Angie's family, standing firmly beside Rob, echoed this sentiment of trust.

Clinton, a town once marked by tranquility, found itself enveloped in shock and despair. The community, however, showed remarkable solidarity, rallying together to support Angie's family and join the search. Flyers with Angie's picture and details about the truck were distributed far and wide. More than 200 volunteers, alongside authorities, embarked on a comprehensive land and air search, scouring Clinton and neighboring counties, but their efforts brought no clue of Angie or the elusive truck.

The case's complexity deepened with the involvement of the state police and FBI, as they sifted through over 1,600 trucks matching the given description. Despite this exhaustive search, the vehicle remained a ghost, evading capture. The local law enforcement agencies united in their efforts, but the trail remained cold.

In a twist of fate, two other haunting cases emerged, echoing similarities with Angie's disappearance. Trudy Darby, a 42-year-old woman, vanished under mysterious circumstances, only to be found murdered days later. Then, there was Sheryl Kenny, a 38-year-old who disappeared from her convenience store job, never to be seen again. These chilling cases formed a geographical triangle with Clinton, igniting theories of a sinister connection.

As years rolled by, Angie's case, once a flurry of activity, began to lose momentum. The FBI withdrew, leaving a lingering sense of unease over Clinton. Rob, wracked with guilt and grief, spiraled into depression, blaming himself for not saving Angie. Angie's parents, Chris and Marsha, struggled to cope with the loss, each finding their own way to endure the unbearable.

Then, in 1994, a glimmer of hope emerged in Trudy Darby's case with the arrest of Marvin Cheney and Jesse Rush. Their gruesome confession to Trudy's murder, however, offered no direct link to Angie's case. Despite Rush's vague allusions to other crimes, no concrete connection to Angie or Sheryl Kenny was established.

Over the years, Angie's disappearance remained an unresolved enigma. A sighting in Manitoba offered a fleeting hope but led nowhere. Then, in 2009, Detective Paul Abbott revealed the existence of potential DNA evidence, rekindling a spark of hope, but this too faded as no new developments surfaced.

The case saw various suspects' names floated, including Kenneth McDuff, a notorious criminal with a dark history. McDuff's brutal past, marked by heinous crimes, added another layer of complexity to the already tangled web of theories surrounding Angie's disappearance.

In a dark twist of fate, Kenneth McDuff's heinous journey through crime escalated to unimaginable cruelty. In a chilling episode, he and his accomplice, Roy Dale Green, targeted three young individuals, including 16-year-old Edna Sullivan. In a night of terror, McDuff mercilessly killed two of the victims in the trunk of a car and then abducted Edna to a secluded spot, where he brutally murdered her using a broomstick.

The duo's barbarity didn't go unnoticed for long. Green, overwhelmed with guilt, confessed, leading to McDuff's arrest and subsequent death sentences. However, McDuff's cunning knew no bounds. Manipulating the system, he convinced the parole board of his coerced participation, leading to an unthinkable parole in 1989. Once free, McDuff's reign of terror resumed, his crimes growing more vicious and sadistic.

On October 10, 1991, McDuff's brutality resurfaced in Waco, Texas, with the abduction of Brenda Thompson. A chance police checkpoint almost thwarted his plans, but McDuff, in a desperate escape, tortured and killed Thompson in a wooded area. His spree of violence continued unchecked until his arrest in 1992 in Kansas City, Missouri.

Despite his numerous confessions to other murders, McDuff remained silent on any involvement in Angela Hammond's abduction. His execution in 1998 ended his reign of terror, but left many questions unanswered, including his potential link to Angie's case, given his proximity in Missouri post her abduction.

The mystery deepened with the emergence of Larry Dewayne Hall, another notorious figure tied to multiple murders. Hall, known for his contradictory confessions, once claimed to have buried victims in the Mark Twain National Forest in Missouri. This revelation sparked speculation about Angie and another missing woman, Sheryl Kenny. Hall's physical resemblance to the description of Angie's abductor fueled these theories.

Then there was Tommy Lynn Sells, executed in 2014 for a series of brutal murders. Sells, known for his preference for petite women and a history of driving stolen pickup trucks, bore a striking resemblance to the "filthy bearded man" Angie described.

As years passed, the memory of Angela Hammond's abduction continued to haunt the town of Clinton. Rob Schaeffer, her fiance, bore the weight of that fateful night, struggling with the trauma of his failed rescue attempt. Detective Damon Parsons and Angie's mother, Marsha Cook, lived with the constant reminder of the unsolved mystery, hoping for a day when answers would finally surface.

In a tale that twists and turns through the corridors of time, the story of Rob Schaeffer and his desperate quest for answers in the disappearance of

Angela Hammond is as heart-wrenching as it is baffling. Despite the shadow of suspicion initially cast upon him, Rob's consistent and unwavering recount of that fateful night never faltered under the intense scrutiny of multiple interrogations and even a lie detector test. His narrative, etched with the pain of loss, remained unchanged, painting a picture of a man engulfed in anguish rather than guilt.

Even 27 years later, the ghost of that night haunts Rob, the 'what ifs' echoing in his mind. His earnest efforts in the search for Angie, coupled with his open participation in the "Unsolved Mysteries" episode, underline a portrait of a man grappling with an unimaginable loss. And yet, despite the relentless investigation by authorities and the unwavering trust of Angie's family, whispers of doubt continue to lurk in some corners, casting aspersions on his innocence.

The narrative of Rob's involvement is riddled with complexities. To believe in his guilt is to accept a scenario of incredible intricacy and precision, executed in a tight window of time by an 18-year-old under immense pressure. Such a theory, while intriguing to some, crumbles under the weight of its own implausibility when held against the timeline of events and Rob's emotional state.

Bill Barker, Angie's former boyfriend, also enters the fray of speculation, with some theorizing a convoluted plot involving both men. Yet, the presence of an unidentified green truck, witnessed independently of Rob's account, casts doubt on such a theory. The logistics of orchestrating such a crime in a small, close-knit community, where the disappearance of a young woman would reverberate with intensity, seem far-fetched at best.

The case then veers into the shadowy realm of notorious criminals – Jessie Rush, Marvin Cheney, Kenneth McDuff, Larry Dewayne Hall, and Tommy Lynn Sells. Each carries a history steeped in violence and depravity, their paths potentially intersecting with Angie's disappearance. Rush and Cheney, tied to a similar crime just miles away, present a sinister possibility. McDuff, a known killer caught in Missouri, Hall, with his web of confessions and recantations, and Sells, with his penchant for petite victims, all fit into the murky puzzle of Angie's fate. Yet, despite the potential connections, hard evidence remains elusive, their involvement a haunting question mark in the annals of unsolved crimes.

The most chilling theory, perhaps, is that of a random act of evil – a stranger passing through Clinton, seizing an opportunity in the dead of night. This theory posits a drifter, unknown to the community, whose path intersected with Angie's in the most tragic of circumstances. The never-found truck, a possible vehicle of abduction and escape, fuels this narrative of a faceless predator who vanished into the night, leaving behind a trail of heartache and unanswered questions.

As the years have passed, the case has grown cold, the leads dwindled, and the hope for new evidence faded. Yet, the pain and the mystery endure, a dark cloud over Clinton and a relentless torment for those who loved Angie. The possibility of forensic evidence, mentioned in 2009, flickers like a distant beacon of hope, yet remains shrouded in uncertainty.

In this labyrinth of theories and suspects, the truth about what happened to Angela Hammond on that fateful night in April remains hidden, locked away in the silence of the unknown. The memory of Angie, a young woman on the brink of a new chapter in her life, now stands as a symbol of a mystery that continues to confound and haunt those who seek justice in the quiet streets of Clinton, Missouri.

Brandi Wells

Brandi Wells, born under the vast Texas sky on November 28, 1982, in the vibrant city of Tyler, carried within her a deep-seated love for music and a fervent dream of one day gracing the stages as a country singer. Her childhood was a melody of aspirations and small-town charms, where she was known as a beacon of musical passion among her peers.

Her educational journey led her to the hallowed halls of Chapel Hill High School. Here, Brandi not only excelled academically but also allowed her ambitions to soar. Her hard work and dedication were rewarded with a prestigious scholarship to the University of Texas, a milestone that marked the beginning of an exciting new chapter in her life.

At university, Brandi's world expanded beyond the realms of academics. She discovered the Flag Corp, an activity that quickly captivated her heart and soul. She devoted countless hours to practice, finding joy and fulfillment in the precision and teamwork it demanded. This pursuit became more than just a pastime; it was a testament to her commitment and a reflection of her spirited personality.

However, life is often a tapestry of unexpected turns. In her second year, Brandi's heart led her down the path of love, culminating in a whirlwind marriage. This new phase brought with it challenges as she struggled to juggle the demands of marriage, university, and work. Ultimately, the delicate balance proved too daunting, and Brandi made the difficult decision to leave university, a choice that echoed with both courage and sacrifice.

The marriage, woven with dreams and hopes, unfortunately unraveled, ending in divorce. This led Brandi on a journey of self-discovery and resilience. She first moved to the bustling city of San Antonio, a place teeming with life and new opportunities. However, it was in the quaint town of Brownsboro where she eventually found solace. At 23, Brandi settled there with a roommate, ready to turn the page and embark on a fresh start.

In Brownsboro, Brandi's aspirations took a new direction. She sent her application to Trinity Valley Community College, where her past dedication to the Flag Corp shone brightly, earning her another scholarship. Her goal was now to nurture young minds; she aspired to become a kindergarten teacher, a role that promised fulfillment and a chance to make a lasting impact on future generations.

Brandi's journey also led her to the local Wal-Mart, where she recently secured a job. Eager to start, she awaited her manager's green light to find a place in the work schedule. Brandi Wells' story is one of resilience, adaptability, and the relentless pursuit of dreams, no matter the twists and turns life may present.

On the warm summer evening of August 2, 2006, Brandi Wells stepped into her mother's apartment, enveloped in the familiar comfort of family and home. Her mother, Ellen Tant, shared this cozy abode with Brandi's younger sister, creating a nest of love and warmth. Ellen, a beacon of support in Brandi's life, listened as her eldest daughter shared her plans for the night: a lively evening out dancing with friends, a much-needed escape into the world of music and rhythm.

As the clock struck 8pm, Brandi, caught in a minor predicament, approached her mother with a request. Her car was almost out of gas, and she wondered if she could borrow Ellen's car for the night's adventure. However, fate would have it that Ellen's car was also low on fuel. After a moment of contemplation, Brandi, driven by the night's promise, decided to brave it with her own vehicle, her spirits undeterred by this small hurdle.

Ellen watched her daughter leave, believing her destination to be the Electric Cowboy, a local club pulsating with energy and familiar faces. But Brandi's night was to take a different turn.

Her first stop was not the club, but a local bowling alley, a place resonant with the echoes of cheers and clattering pins. Here, a family friend tended the bar, a familiar and friendly face in the midst of the alley's lively atmosphere. Brandi, maintaining her usual charm, bought a single drink, putting it on her mother's tab—a small gesture of familial bond and trust.

It was here that Brandi revealed her true destination for the night: Grand Central Station, a popular spot located about 45 minutes away in Longview. This revelation brought a note of concern from the family friend. The distance, coupled with the fact that Brandi was venturing out alone, painted a picture of potential risk. The friend, their worry evident, tried to dissuade Brandi from this solitary journey. But Brandi, ever independent and determined, was resolute in her plans.

Unbeknownst to them, this decision would set the course for a night that would unfold into a tapestry of mystery and unanswered questions. Brandi, with her spirit of adventure and love for life, stepped out into the night, unknowingly walking into a chapter of her life that would leave a lasting imprint on the hearts of those who knew her.

As dawn broke on August 3, 2006, a scene unfolded on the side of Interstate 20 that would soon become a critical piece in a perplexing puzzle. Around 9:15 am, a vigilant highway trooper's eyes were drawn to a 2000 Black Pontiac Grand Prix, sitting abandoned, a solitary figure against the vast expanse of the road. The trooper, trained to notice the out-of-place, approached the vehicle.

He meticulously ran the license plate through his system, searching for clues in the sea of data. The car's silent story revealed no immediate alarms; there were no records of it having been stolen. Following protocol, he tagged it as abandoned and continued on his patrol, unaware of the gravity this vehicle held in the tapestry of a family's life.

Meanwhile, Ellen Tant, Brandi's mother, was greeting the new day in her apartment, the morning light bringing a sense of peace. However, a subtle unease began to creep in as she noticed the absence of her daughter, Brandi, who had not yet returned from her night out. Ellen's mind, seasoned with the patience and understanding of a mother, did not leap to panic. She reasoned that perhaps Brandi had indulged a bit too much and decided to stay with a friend for safety.

As the day leisurely unfolded, an unexpected call pierced the calm. It was from Brandi's roommate, expressing concern. Brandi had been expected back in Brownsboro that afternoon, and her absence was out of character. Ellen, now with a seed of worry sprouting in her heart, reached for her phone and dialed Brandi's number, only to be greeted by the impersonal tone of voicemail. Still, Ellen clung to hope, telling herself there was a logical explanation for Brandi's silence.

The tick of the clock marked the passage of time, and with each passing hour, Ellen's concern deepened. By August 4, with Brandi still unreachable, Ellen's maternal instincts transformed into action. She made her way to the Tyler Police Department, her steps heavy with the weight of uncertainty. It was there, in the midst of her growing apprehension, that she learned from her youngest daughter a crucial detail: Brandi hadn't gone to the Electric Cowboy as initially believed, but to Grand Central Station.

Armed with this new information, Ellen, driven by a mother's unyielding resolve, set out for Longview. Her eyes searched the club's parking lot and the surrounding areas, hoping for any sign, any clue that might lead her to Brandi.

But the silent streets and empty spaces offered no answers, no whispers of her daughter's whereabouts.

Then, on August 5, the complexity of the situation escalated. Ellen was informed that the Longview Police Department would be taking over the case. The reality of the situation was setting in; this was no ordinary delay or miscommunication. Ellen was now in the throes of a parent's worst nightmare. With a heavy heart, she prepared to file a missing person's report with them, stepping into a journey filled with uncertainty.

On the morning of August 6, 2006, the quiet routine of the police force was interrupted by a call that would add a new dimension to an unfolding mystery. A concerned citizen, vigilant in their daily commute, reported something unusual: the 2000 Black Pontiac Grand Prix, still resting abandoned on the side of Interstate 20, untouched and silent as if holding its breath. The police, sensing the significance of this vehicle, quickly linked it to the increasingly concerning case of Brandi Wells.

Two days later, on August 8, the scene around the abandoned car transformed into a hive of investigative activity. CSI professionals and cadaver dogs were summoned, their expertise crucial in uncovering any hidden truths. The dogs, with their keen sense of smell, scoured the area, but the scent of the missing woman remained elusive, as if swept away by the winds of mystery. The investigators, too, found no evidence of a struggle in the vicinity of the car. However, a seemingly innocuous discovery inside the vehicle piqued their interest: a napkin bearing a man's name and number.

The police, following this slender thread, contacted the man. He proved to be an open book, willingly sharing the details of his brief encounter with Brandi on the night she vanished. He recalled offering to buy her a drink, an offer she politely declined, instead requesting some gas money. After a short interaction, their paths diverged, leaving behind more questions than answers. Despite the intrigue of this encounter, the police did not view him as a suspect in Brandi's disappearance.

Recognizing the complexity of the case, the Longview Police Department sought reinforcements. The FBI was called in, adding their extensive resources and expertise to the search for Brandi.

Further examination of Brandi's car only deepened the enigma. The driver's seat was pushed back far beyond Brandi's reach, suggesting someone much taller than her diminutive 5'0" stature had last driven the car. The vehicle's position, angled peculiarly and abandoned some 400 to 500 yards from the exit leading back towards Tyler, painted a picture of haste and interruption. Inside, the keys were missing, and the driver's door was left ajar, as if the last occupant had departed in a hurry.

Amidst these perplexing clues, Brandi's purse was found in the car, along with a cellphone initially believed to be hers. A gas can, a silent witness to unknown events, sat in the trunk. However, her family cast doubt on its belonging to Brandi.

The investigative lens then shifted to the surveillance footage of Grand Central Station. The team discovered that Brandi's driver's license had been swiped at the club around 10:44 pm on August 2. In a heart-wrenching task, Brandi's family was brought in to scrutinize the footage, searching for a face they so dearly missed. Amidst the grainy images, they identified a woman they believed to be Brandi. She was not alone; men accompanied her. This revelation spurred a public plea, a call for information about these unidentified individuals, in the hope that they might hold the key to unraveling the mystery of Brandi Wells' disappearance.

As the investigation into Brandi Wells' mysterious disappearance intensified, the police sought to piece together the events of that fateful night at Grand Central Station. Through conversations with the staff who were on duty, a clearer picture began to emerge. Brandi, it was discovered, had made multiple calls to the club that night, seeking directions. Once there, she appeared to maintain a low profile, ordering at most a single drink. This revelation added another layer to the unfolding mystery, suggesting Brandi's visit to the club was more complicated than initially thought.

Ten days into the search, a significant development occurred. Brandi's mother, ever proactive in the search for her daughter, provided investigators with a sample of Brandi's DNA, a crucial step in aiding the investigation. During this process, she made a startling observation. The cellphone that the police had in evidence, previously believed to be Brandi's, was actually that of an ex-boyfriend who was deployed overseas. This discovery explained why only a few contacts in the phone's address book were familiar with Brandi. In response to this twist, the police swiftly moved to subpoena Brandi's cell phone records, hoping to find a lead within the digital footprints of her communications.

However, Brandi's family, driven by urgency and determination, was not content to simply wait for the subpoena. They reached out to a friend of Brandi who shared a cellphone contract with her. The friend, cooperating fully, sent over the records, revealing that there was no suspicious activity prior to Brandi's disappearance. But about nine days following her vanishing, the records showed calls that piqued the investigators' interest, hinting at potential leads.

The calls were traced to two individuals, who were promptly brought in for questioning. Their testimonies led the police to a potential person of interest - a man who claimed to have found the cellphone on the side of the road, about a week after Brandi went missing. This area, situated on the south side of town and notorious for drug and sex trafficking, was alarmingly close to where Brandi's car had been abandoned. The man's story, however, was riddled with inconsistencies, changing with each telling. When offered a polygraph test by the FBI, he initially refused but later agreed, only to fail the test. The two individuals initially questioned, on the other hand, passed their polygraph tests. Despite this, the man was not considered a person of interest in Brandi's disappearance.

Meanwhile, Brandi's family, fueled by a mix of hope and desperation, launched a fervent campaign to keep her case in the public eye. They initiated a chain email, tirelessly reached out to local newspapers, and kept in constant touch with television stations, doing everything in their power to ensure Brandi's story remained alive in the hearts and minds of the community.

Six weeks into the investigation, despite the tireless efforts of both the family and law enforcement, the trail began to grow cold. Leads that once seemed promising dried up, and the case tragically shifted into the realm of cold cases.

In a relentless quest for answers, Ellen Tant, Brandi's mother, immersed herself in the examination of the Grand Central Station's surveillance footage, determined to uncover any clue that might lead to her daughter. Her meticulous scrutiny led to a startling revelation: the girl initially identified as Brandi in the footage was, in fact, not her. The clothes she wore differed from those Brandi had donned when she left the apartment on the evening of August 2, 2006, a detail that only a mother's keen eye could catch.

Brandi's aunt and uncle joined Ellen in this painstaking review, their collective efforts fueled by hope and desperation. Their diligence paid off when they spotted Brandi on the surveillance tape, entering the club at 10:35 pm. The earlier misidentification had been a result of the surveillance camera's inaccurate time stamp. The footage revealed Brandi arriving alone and leaving around 12:30 am. However, since the camera only captured the entrance, what transpired after Brandi exited the frame remained shrouded in mystery.

On September 19, 2006, with the investigation seemingly at a standstill, Brandi's family reached out to the Laura Recovery Centre, an organization dedicated to assisting in the search for missing persons. The Centre swiftly organized a search operation on September 26, deploying volunteers on horseback and four-wheelers. They scoured the area around Grand Central Station, accompanied by cadaver dogs, in a thorough and hopeful effort to uncover any trace of Brandi. Despite their extensive efforts, the search yielded no tangible results.

The case took a harrowing turn on October 29, 2006. In the oilfields of Gregg County, approximately seven miles from where Brandi's car had been found, the burning body of a woman was discovered. The condition of the body made identification a challenge, but police noted the woman was wearing a purple sweater and blue jeans. An autopsy confirmed she was a white female, and a forensic artist was brought in to create a rendering, hoping someone might recognize her. Initially thought to be Brandi, this theory was later dispelled by dental records. The woman, hauntingly referred to as "Lavender Doe," was finally identified as Dana Dodd in February 2019.

The search for Brandi continued with unwavering determination. On December 23, 2006, the Laura Recovery Centre conducted a second search. A bag of bones was discovered, a grim find that initially sparked hope, but was later confirmed to be of animal origin.

A third search effort unfolded in early 2007, but again, no clues emerged.

In a twist that reignited a flicker of hope, Ellen received a mysterious call in 2010. A man, identifying himself as Tim, claimed that Brandi was alive in Kansas City, Missouri. The call, abrupt and tantalizingly brief, ended before Ellen could extract any further information, leaving her with more questions than answers.

In a relentless quest for answers, Ellen Tant, Brandi's mother, immersed herself in the examination of the Grand Central Station's surveillance footage, determined to uncover any clue that might lead to her daughter. Her meticulous scrutiny led to a startling revelation: the girl initially identified as Brandi in the footage was, in fact, not her. The clothes she wore differed from those Brandi had donned when she left the apartment on the evening of August 2, 2006, a detail that only a mother's keen eye could catch.

Brandi's aunt and uncle joined Ellen in this painstaking review, their collective efforts fueled by hope and desperation. Their diligence paid off when they spotted Brandi on the surveillance tape, entering the club at 10:35 pm. The earlier misidentification had been a result of the surveillance camera's inaccurate time stamp. The footage revealed Brandi arriving alone and leaving around 12:30 am. However, since the camera only captured the entrance, what transpired after Brandi exited the frame remained shrouded in mystery.

On September 19, 2006, with the investigation seemingly at a standstill, Brandi's family reached out to the Laura Recovery Centre, an organization dedicated to assisting in the search for missing persons. The Centre swiftly organized a search operation on September 26, deploying volunteers on horseback and four-wheelers. They scoured the area around Grand Central Station, accompanied by cadaver dogs, in a thorough and hopeful effort to uncover any trace of Brandi. Despite their extensive efforts, the search yielded no tangible results.

The case took a harrowing turn on October 29, 2006. In the oilfields of Gregg County, approximately seven miles from where Brandi's car had been found, the burning body of a woman was discovered. The condition of the body made identification a challenge, but police noted the woman was wearing a purple sweater and blue jeans. An autopsy confirmed she was a white female, and a forensic artist was brought in to create a rendering, hoping someone might recognize her. Initially thought to be Brandi, this theory was later dispelled by dental records. The woman, hauntingly referred to as "Lavender Doe," was finally identified as Dana Dodd in February 2019.

The search for Brandi continued with unwavering determination. On December 23, 2006, the Laura Recovery Centre conducted a second search. A bag of bones was discovered, a grim find that initially sparked hope, but was later confirmed to be of animal origin.

A third search effort unfolded in early 2007, but again, no clues emerged.

In a twist that reignited a flicker of hope, Ellen received a mysterious call in 2010. A man, identifying himself as Tim, claimed that Brandi was alive in Kansas City, Missouri. The call, abrupt and tantalizingly brief, ended before Ellen could extract any further information, leaving her with more questions than answers. This enigmatic call, though a glimmer of hope, added another layer of complexity to the enduring mystery of Brandi Wells' disappearance.

Jamie Fraley

Jamie Fraley's story unfolds with haunting mystery and tragic undertones, rooted in the quiet town of Gastonia, North Carolina. At just 22 years old, Jamie's vibrant life was abruptly overshadowed by a chilling disappearance that still remains unsolved. The events leading up to her vanishing began to unravel in the early hours of April 8, 2008, leaving a community in dismay and a family seeking answers.

Living in the Copperfield apartment complex on Alloway Festa Road, Jamie was a stone's throw away from my own location, establishing a personal connection to her tale. Her aspirations were admirable; she was a student at Gaston College, ardently working towards a career as a substance abuse counselor. Unfortunately, this dream was snatched away in the most bewildering circumstances.

The day before she disappeared, on April 7th, Jamie was struck by what seemed to be a severe case of stomach flu. Her condition was so alarming that it necessitated two separate hospital visits within a single day. Without a driver's license, Jamie depended heavily on her friends, neighbors, and social services for transportation. Her first trip to the hospital that morning was brief, and she was soon sent home.

Upon her return, a friend, who had been entrusted with dog-sitting duties, visited Jamie. This friend not only collected the dog but also kindly offered to handle Jamie's prescription, a small yet significant gesture of support. Despite this help, Jamie's condition did not improve. Convinced that her illness was more serious, she made a second trip to the hospital later that day.

This time, she turned to Ricky Simmons Sr. for assistance. Jamie was engaged to Ricky Simmons Jr., who had been dating her since 2006. However, in 2007, he was incarcerated for a 15-month sentence due to theft charges, leaving his father, who lived just two doors down from Jamie in the same apartment complex and worked there as a maintenance worker, to look after her needs. Ricky Sr. dutifully drove her to the hospital, but reports vary on whether he or a friend brought her back.

Returning home late that afternoon, Jamie continued to struggle with her health. By midnight, convinced that her symptoms were far more serious than initially thought, she reached out to her mother, expressing her urgent need to return to the hospital, fearing that her condition was deteriorating into something far graver than just stomach flu.

As these puzzling events unfolded, what transpired after this phone call to her mother remains shrouded in mystery. The question of what truly happened to Jamie Fraley and her current whereabouts remains unanswered, casting a shadow of intrigue and sorrow over her story.

On the fateful night of April 8th, around 1:30 a.m., Jamie Fraley found herself in a distressing situation, grappling with what she believed to be more than just a stomach flu. In the stillness of the night, she reached out to a friend over the phone, sharing her ordeal. Jamie detailed her persistent sickness and her two previous trips to the hospital, conveying her growing conviction that her illness was gravely serious. She anxiously awaited a ride to the hospital for a third time, hoping for answers and relief.

As the conversation progressed, Jamie abruptly cut it short, indicating that her ride had arrived. Mysteriously, she didn't disclose the identity of the driver, referring to them only as "he". With those parting words, the call ended, marking the last time anyone would hear from Jamie.

The subsequent day, Jamie uncharacteristically missed a crucial meeting. Concerned, her family, already aware of her poor health, grew increasingly worried due to her silence post her intended hospital visit. Driven by a mix of concern and fear, they decided to check on her at her residence, fearing that her condition might have worsened.

Upon arriving at Jamie's home, they were met with eerie silence. The door was locked, but once they gained access, a troubling scene unfolded. Inside, they found Jamie's personal belongings - her purse, ID, and money, all untouched. Strikingly, only two items were missing: Jamie herself, and her cell phone. The lack of any signs of struggle and the locked door painted a confusing picture. Initially, they thought she might still be at the hospital, perhaps detained for overnight observation due to the severity of her illness.

Clutching onto this hope, Jamie's family rushed to the hospital, only to be met with a chilling revelation: Jamie had never arrived for her third visit. This realization struck a harrowing chord – Jamie had vanished into the unknown somewhere between her apartment and the hospital.

Desperation set in as her family and friends launched a frantic search, scouring every possible location to find her. Days turned into weeks with no sign of Jamie, no leads to her whereabouts, and no clues to unravel the mystery of her disappearance.

The mysterious disappearance of Jamie Fraley immediately set off alarm bells, prompting her family to report her as a missing person. Recognizing the gravity of the situation, the Gaston County Police launched a substantial investigation without delay. Three dedicated investigators were assigned to work full-time on the case, alongside the state's Bureau of Investigations and the FBI. The involvement of such high-profile agencies underscored the seriousness of Jamie's case and the growing suspicion of foul play.

Two days after Jamie's last known contact, a significant clue emerged. Utility workers stumbled upon her phone at the intersection of South New Hope Road and East Hudson Boulevard, only a few miles from her home. This discovery could have been a major breakthrough, but by the time authorities arrived, multiple people had handled the phone, contaminating potential forensic evidence like fingerprints and DNA. Investigators were forced to pivot their focus to the phone's contents.

An analysis of the phone revealed several calls made around 4:30 a.m., but authorities eventually concluded these calls were unrelated to Jamie's disappearance. The nature of these calls, made from her phone, suggested that perhaps someone else had possession of her phone, either discarding it after use or using it to contact others. The most intriguing detail, however, was an incoming call to Jamie's phone at 5:00 a.m., just half an hour later. The origin of this call remained a mystery, adding another layer of complexity to the case.

Attention quickly turned to potential suspects. Jamie's fiancé, Ricky Simmons Jr., was incarcerated at the time, eliminating him as a suspect. However, the focus shifted to Ricky Simmons Sr., Jamie's future father-in-law. According to investigators, he was the last known person to have seen Jamie that day. This detail raised several questions: Did he accompany Jamie to and from the hospital that second time, or was he the one who picked her up that night? The ambiguity around these points fueled further investigation.

Ricky Sr.'s past painted a troubling picture. He had a criminal record that included a six-year prison sentence for manslaughter in the 1980s, having strangled a girlfriend to death. Additionally, he had a history of protective orders filed against him by other girlfriends. His proximity to Jamie's apartment and an alleged obsession with her further incriminated him in the eyes of the investigators. When asked to take a polygraph test, he refused, which could be interpreted as self-protection or a sign of guilt.

Authorities strongly suspected Ricky Sr.'s involvement in Jamie's disappearance and worked diligently to build a case against him. However, their efforts to link him directly to the case were dramatically hindered two months after Jamie vanished, leaving the investigation at a critical and uncertain juncture.

The perplexing case of Jamie Fraley's disappearance took a bizarre and tragic turn on June 7th. An ex-girlfriend of Ricky Simmons Sr., who had recently sought a protective order against him, began to notice an odd and unpleasant smell emanating from her car. Initially dismissing it as something trivial, perhaps a forgotten item, she couldn't pinpoint the source. However, by June 8th, the smell had intensified to an unbearable level, prompting a thorough investigation of her vehicle.

The discovery she made in the trunk of her car was nothing short of horrifying. To her utter shock and dismay, she found the lifeless body of Ricky Simmons Sr. The police were immediately summoned to the scene, and a chilling narrative began to unfold, piecing together the last moments of Ricky Sr.'s life.

Investigators deduced a probable scenario: Ricky Sr., harboring resentment over the protective order, had broken into her car using a set of keys he had obtained. Two weeks prior, her car had been burglarized, and an extra set of keys stolen from her bag – likely by Ricky Sr. Fueled by anger and perhaps planning a sinister act of revenge, he used these keys to hide in the trunk, intending to ambush her.

However, his plan went awry. The ex-girlfriend delayed using her car, and during this time, the weather was swelteringly hot, with temperatures around 90 degrees. Trapped in the trunk with no ventilation, Ricky Sr. likely succumbed to the extreme heat. Confusion and delirium would have set in, causing him to forget or overlook the emergency trunk release. The tragic conclusion was that he died of heatstroke, an unintended victim of his own vengeful plot.

This turn of events was a devastating blow to the investigation into Jamie's disappearance. Ricky Sr. was the primary person of interest, and with his death, potential leads or confessions he might have provided vanished. Both Jamie's family and the Simmons family expressed their belief that Ricky Sr. held crucial information about Jamie's fate. Jamie's mother recalled her reaction to this news; the moment she learned of Ricky Sr.'s death, she was overwhelmed with despair, feeling as though any hope of finding answers about her daughter had been irretrievably lost.

When Ricky Simmons Jr. was released from jail, he found himself thrust into a whirlwind of tragic events. Not only had his fiancée disappeared under mysterious circumstances, but his father had also died in such a bizarre and unexpected manner. The media and public scrutiny only added to his distress. Overwhelmed by grief and the rapid succession of traumatic events, Ricky Jr. expressed his belief that his father might have known more about Jamie's disappearance. This suspicion hinted at his awareness of his father's possible obsession with Jamie.

Ricky Jr. faced an immense challenge, coping with the loss of the two most important people in his life in such a short span. His struggle to process and grieve these losses was palpable. Members of the Simmons family also came forward, echoing the sentiment that Ricky Sr. might have been involved in Jamie's disappearance, further deepening the mystery and the tragedy that had befallen both families.

The perplexing case of Jamie Fraley's disappearance has left authorities and those close to her grappling with the painful acceptance that she may no longer be alive. With Ricky Simmons Sr.'s untimely death, the investigation hit a significant roadblock, leaving a trail of unanswered questions and theories in its wake.

The most prominent theory revolves around Ricky Simmons Sr. His past behavior and the circumstances leading up to his death paint a picture of a man with a troubled history, particularly in his relationships with women. Reports suggested that Ricky Sr. was deeply infatuated, even obsessed, with Jamie, which was unsettling given her profound love for his son, Ricky Jr. The intensity of Jamie and Ricky Jr.'s relationship, symbolized by their mutual tattoos and rapid engagement, might have ignited feelings of jealousy or resentment in Ricky Sr.

Ricky Sr.'s difficulties in life seemed to center around his relationships with women, marked by a pattern of being rejected and subsequently reacting with hostility. His son's successful and passionate relationship with Jamie might have been perceived as a personal affront, fueling his anger and possible fixation on her. This theory posits that Ricky Sr. might have seen in Jamie the kind of partner he felt he deserved but was continually denied.

The possibility that Ricky Sr. may have acted on these feelings is heightened by his proximity to Jamie, living just two doors away. He might have attempted to approach Jamie, only to be rejected due to her loyalty to his son. Such a rejection could have been a significant blow to his ego, potentially leading to drastic actions.

One intriguing aspect of this theory is the nature of Jamie's illness. Her repeated hospital visits for what seemed like a worsening stomach flu raise suspicions. Could Ricky Sr. have been responsible, possibly poisoning her? His role as a maintenance worker at the apartment complex provided him with the means to access her apartment and tamper with her food or water. The deterioration of Jamie's condition throughout the day, rather than improvement, lends some credence to this hypothesis.

The mysterious circumstances of her final departure to the hospital further compound the mystery. Whoever was responsible for her disappearance made a decisive intervention that night, altering her intended course to seek medical help. The question remains: why would Ricky Sr., living so close, take an hour and a half to pick her up if he was indeed involved? This delay raises doubts about his direct involvement in her disappearance at that specific moment.

Consider this chilling scenario: What if the person who was with Jamie in the car that fateful night forcibly seized her phone and callously threw it out of the window? The discovery of her phone at the intersection of South New Hope Road and East Hudson Boulevard could offer a sinister explanation. While some may question the workers in the area, it's more plausible that the phone was deliberately discarded to prevent Jamie from reaching out for help.

The peculiar aspect of this theory lies in the timing of certain phone calls. Jamie was last known to have talked to someone around 1:30 in the morning, but calls were made from her phone at 4:30 a.m. Given the short distance between her apartment complex and the location where her phone was found, it's unlikely that someone casually strolling by would pick it up. The area around the intersection lacks significant foot traffic, with only a Sonic restaurant nearby. This raises the possibility that whoever took Jamie may have intentionally tossed her phone there.

What adds a layer of intrigue to this theory is the geographical context. If you continue straight on East Hudson Boulevard, you'd eventually reach a substantial state park. Alternatively, turning south off East Hudson would lead to the vast Catawba River. Both routes provide ample opportunities to dispose of evidence. Numerous bridges and secluded spots along the way offer potential hiding places for a tragic secret.

The question that lingers is whether these areas were thoroughly searched. With a two-hour window from Jamie's last known contact at 1:30 a.m. to the 4:30 a.m. phone calls, it's entirely conceivable that someone could have driven to one of these locations, taken Jamie's phone, placed calls to create a facade of normalcy, and then discarded the phone. This theory challenges the assumption that Jamie walked away on her own, emphasizing the possibility of foul play.

While many firmly believe that Ricky Simmons Sr. had a role in Jamie's disappearance, given his jealous, obsessive, and violent tendencies, it's important to consider alternative scenarios. The circumstances surrounding Jamie's phone raise questions that demand answers. The haunting mystery of Jamie Fraley's vanishing continues to perplex and disturb those seeking the truth about her fate.

Jeremy Carl Bert

Jeremy Carl Bert's life journey is a tapestry woven with vibrant threads of adventure, resilience, and mystery. Born on June 18, 1973, in the heartwarming town of American Falls, Idaho, he was the beloved son of Van and Cheryl Bert. From his early days, Jeremy was a bundle of energy, a boy whose spirit was as boundless as the Idaho skies. His parents often reminisced about his fun-loving nature, his outgoing personality, and his knack for making friends easily. Jeremy's childhood was marked by a diagnosis of ADHD, yet he never let it define him. Instead, he channeled his boundless energy into pursuits that would shape his character.

High school was a pivotal time for Jeremy. He discovered his love for sports, finding an outlet for his energy in the rhythmic pounding of feet on the track and the adrenaline rush of football games. His high school years weren't just about sports; they were about finding himself, about turning challenges into opportunities.

After graduating, Jeremy took a bold step in service to his country. He joined the United States Navy, a decision that reflected his deep sense of patriotism and adventure. For six years, he served in the Gulf War, an experience that was both challenging and enriching. His naval journey took him to exotic locales like the Persian Gulf, Japan, and Australia, broadening his horizons and fueling his adventurous spirit.

During his time in Japan, Jeremy's life took a romantic turn. He met Raina, and their love blossomed amidst the backdrop of naval ships and foreign shores. They married in a unique ceremony on a naval ship, a testament to their unconventional and passionate relationship. However, upon returning to the States, their marriage faced turbulent waters and eventually, Raina returned to Japan, leaving their relationship in a state of separation, not quite ended but no longer thriving.

Back home in Idaho, Jeremy's life seemed to be on a positive trajectory. He transitioned from military life to civilian life, channeling his discipline and energy into building a successful roofing business. He embraced fatherhood with the birth of his daughter, McKenzie, a shining light in his life. To the outside world, Jeremy had everything: a thriving business, a loving family, and a zest for life. He was an avid hunter, someone who found peace and exhilaration in the great outdoors, in the pursuit of elk amidst the vast wilderness.

But then, the unexpected happened. On the night of February 11, 2007, at 10:30 p.m., Jeremy's story took a mysterious turn. After leaving his daughter in the care of his father, Van, with plans to dine with a friend and discuss hunting grounds, Jeremy vanished. He never made it to either friend's house, and he never returned home. This sudden disappearance left a void, an unsolved puzzle that begged for answers.

As we delve deeper into Jeremy's story, we find a man of many layers, a man whose life was a blend of joy, adventure, challenges, and unexplained mysteries. His time in the Navy, particularly in Japan, was more than just a chapter in his service; it was a chapter in his heart, one that brought him love, albeit a love that couldn't withstand the tests of distance and time.

Jeremy's life is a story that resonates with the vibrancy of his personality and the enigma of his disappearance. It's a story that reminds us of the complexities of human life and the unpredictable paths our journeys can take.

The love story of Jeremy and Kim George is a captivating tale of passion, complexity, and heartache, unfolding against the backdrop of the ever-changing landscapes of Idaho. Their relationship, as recounted by Jeremy's family, was a rollercoaster of intense emotions, marked by soaring highs and profound lows. It was a romance that burned brightly, fueled by a deep, passionate connection.

Their story began in Pocatello, Idaho, where the first sparks of their love ignited. Kim, in her interviews, reminisced about the moment she met Jeremy, feeling an instant, profound connection. She knew then that her love for him would be a lasting one. However, the couple soon realized that their future lay elsewhere, and they set their sights on Boise. It was a city that promised new beginnings and ample opportunities, especially for Jeremy's entrepreneurial spirit.

In Boise, Jeremy embarked on a new venture, launching his own contracting business. His expertise in roof repair and replacement quickly turned this endeavor into a profitable venture. Together, Jeremy and Kim built a life in Boise, purchasing a home and laying down roots. David, Jeremy's cousin and best friend, fondly recalled the early days of their relationship, describing how Jeremy was utterly captivated by Kim, falling for her "hook, line, and sinker."

The narrative took an exciting turn in late 2001 when Kim discovered she was pregnant. The news filled them with joy and anticipation. It was a pivotal moment for Jeremy, who decided it was time to close the chapter of his life with Raina and start anew with Kim. Their quest for a divorce lawyer led them to Genie Braun, a proficient attorney in family court and divorce matters. Jeremy and Genie's professional relationship, however, soon sparked concerns.

David noted in interviews that Jeremy seemed infatuated with Genie from the onset, drawn to her poise and elegance. This budding connection coincided with a tragic turn in Jeremy and Kim's life – a miscarriage that left them both shattered. Jeremy's profound sorrow found expression in a poignant poem he wrote about the child they lost, a testament to his deep emotional capacity.

May 2002 marked a significant milestone as Jeremy's divorce was finalized. Yet, his interactions with Genie continued, sowing seeds of doubt in Kim's mind. Kim, reflecting on this period, admitted to sensing an undercurrent of something more than friendship between Jeremy and Genie. The situation grew more complex as Genie started bestowing Jeremy with lavish gifts and dinners, blurring the lines between professional and personal.

Despite the undercurrents of doubt and complexity, Jeremy and Kim's relationship progressed. By August 2002, when they tied the knot, Kim was three months pregnant. It was a bittersweet moment, as Jeremy confided in his brother Shane after the ceremony. He expressed uncertainty about his readiness for marriage, yet felt it was the right step with a baby on the way.

The birth of his daughter McKenzie was a transformative moment for Jeremy. When he first gazed into her eyes, he was overwhelmed with an indescribable love. Cheryl, Jeremy's mother, fondly recalled how he would call McKenzie his perfect little angel, a testament to the profound impact she had on his life. However, this deep paternal bond was not enough to untangle the intricate web of his romantic life.

Despite his newfound fatherly love, Jeremy continued his romantic involvement with Genie, unable to sever the ties that bound them. This continued liaison led to a heart-wrenching revelation for Kim just three weeks after McKenzie's birth. Confronting the painful truth, she asked Jeremy to leave their home. The turbulence in their relationship hastened its end, and before their first anniversary, Jeremy and Kim were divorced.

Yet, the story did not end there. Jeremy maintained romantic relationships with both Kim and Genie, a complicated love triangle that persisted despite his inability to commit to one. Kim, reflecting on those times, acknowledged

Jeremy's devotion as a father. He cherished every moment with McKenzie, for whom he would go to great lengths to be with. She was, as Jeremy often said, the most important part of his life.

The dramatic arc of Jeremy's life took a sharp turn in 2004 when his relationship with Genie came to an abrupt and shocking end. Jeremy found himself in the midst of a legal storm, testifying against Genie before a grand jury. Genie was embroiled in serious legal trouble, accused of forgery, influencing a witness, and destroying evidence in a child custody case. It was a revelation that deeply affected Jeremy, leading him to devise a plan to ensure Genie faced justice for her actions.

In a move that surprised many, Jeremy came back to Kim, confessing his plan to continue seeing Genie only to gather evidence against her. He secretly recorded their conversations, collecting incriminating evidence that would be pivotal in Genie's conviction. Genie was sentenced to a year in county jail and 14 years of probation.

Following Genie's conviction, Kim and Jeremy began a cautious journey toward reconciliation. Despite the complexities of their past, they were united in their love for McKenzie and the desire to provide a stable environment for her. They moved into an apartment with Van, Jeremy's father, in an attempt to rebuild their relationship. Kim even considered retrieving her ring, a symbol of hope for a renewed future together.

Throughout this period, Jeremy and Genie's interactions continued sporadically. Van observed that Genie would often bring lunch to him and Jeremy at job sites. However, at some point, Jeremy asked Genie to distance herself, a decision indicative of his shifting priorities.

As 2007 dawned, the dynamic between Kim and Jeremy showed signs of improvement. They were making concerted efforts to work on their relationship, driven by their mutual commitment to being exemplary parents for McKenzie.

She was the bond that kept them connected, the shared love that anchored them amidst the storms of their past. But as they navigated these waters, the currents of fate were about to take an unexpected turn, leading to Jeremy's mysterious disappearance.

On that fateful Sunday, February 11th, 2007, the tranquility of Kim's world began to unravel in a series of unexpected events. She left Boise for a week-long seminar in Las Vegas, a routine work commitment that soon turned into the backdrop of a perplexing mystery involving her partner, Jeremy. Meanwhile, Jeremy had been visiting family in American Falls, a trip that was part of their regular life rhythm. Upon his return to Boise, he made a point to check in with Kim, ensuring she had arrived safely in Vegas. Their conversation was brief, but nothing seemed amiss at the time.

With Valentine's Day on the horizon, Kim playfully suggested that Jeremy take a break from his busy schedule and join her in Vegas, even if just for a day. Jeremy, however, insisted that his workload was too heavy to allow for such a getaway. According to Van, Jeremy's father, after returning home, Jeremy spent some time on his computer before dressing up and announcing his plan to visit a friend to discuss potential elk hunting locations. He left the apartment, taking Kim's car, and entrusted Van with putting their daughter McKenzie to bed.

The next day, February 12th, Kim was immersed in her seminar activities, her mind occupied with the tasks at hand. It wasn't until she returned to her hotel room that evening that she realized she hadn't checked in with Jeremy. As she walked into her room, her phone rang, displaying Jeremy's caller ID. Excitedly, she answered, "Hey babe," but the call abruptly disconnected. Subsequent attempts to reach Jeremy were met with his voicemail, leaving Kim puzzled but not overly concerned.

The following day, as Kim continued with her classes, a startling text message from Jeremy arrived around 2 p.m. The message read, "We need to talk" –

four words that no partner ever wants to hear. Engulfed in her seminar, Kim couldn't immediately respond. By 5 p.m., when she finally had a moment to check her phone, she found 17 additional messages from Jeremy, each more alarming than the last. The messages ranged from farewells and wishes of good luck to declarations of leaving to start a new life and plans to collect McKenzie later. Kim was stunned. This barrage of texts seemed utterly out of character for Jeremy, who typically preferred direct phone conversations for important matters.

Fearing the worst, Kim desperately texted back, seeking clarification and understanding. After a tense wait, Jeremy replied, and a back-and-forth texting ensued into the evening. Kim's mind raced with questions and doubts. Was it really Jeremy on the other end of these messages? Why would he choose to communicate such critical decisions through texts? And most importantly, what prompted this sudden, drastic change in his behavior?

In a final attempt to reach clarity, Kim called Jeremy's phone multiple times. When he finally answered, she pleaded with him not to make any hasty decisions. All she heard in response was a heavy sigh before the line went dead once again. Confusion and devastation engulfed Kim. She couldn't fathom why Jeremy would suddenly distance himself like this. Was Genie Braun somehow involved in this unexpected turn of events? The pieces just didn't fit together. Kim's heart was breaking, not only for herself but for the uncertainty this brought into their daughter McKenzie's life.

Kim's concern for Jeremy's sudden and uncharacteristic behavior propelled her to reach out to Van, Jeremy's father, hoping to glean some insight into the situation. Van, equally puzzled by Jeremy's absence, had assumed his son was off on one of his usual solitary excursions - a hike or a hunting trip to clear his mind. However, when Kim shared the disturbing content of Jeremy's texts, Van was at a loss. It seemed inconceivable to him that Jeremy would abandon McKenzie, the center of his world.

Determined to unravel the mystery, Kim next reached out to David, Jeremy's cousin and closest confidant. If anyone was privy to Jeremy's state of mind or recent activities, it would be David. David's bewilderment matched that of Kim and Van. He had spent time with Jeremy just days before, enjoying a typical weekend of beers, cards, and bar-hopping in their hometown of American Falls. Nothing in Jeremy's demeanor during that weekend had hinted at the turmoil that would soon unfold.

As Kim relayed the baffling messages, David recalled Jeremy's sudden desire to leave a bar in Pocatello, wanting to find a quieter place to talk. However, Jeremy had departed alone as David was waiting for someone else. Now, with the knowledge of Jeremy's cryptic messages and abrupt disappearance, David couldn't reconcile the Jeremy he knew with the actions being described. It was unthinkable that Jeremy would contemplate a new life away from his beloved daughter.

The situation took a more alarming turn when Kim revealed the personal nature of the remaining 17 texts. They echoed the affectionate exchanges between Jeremy and McKenzie, including their endearing ritual where McKenzie would credit her cuteness to her father. The texts seemed carefully crafted to convince Kim of their authenticity.

Upon returning from Vegas, Kim's unease deepened. Not only was Jeremy missing, but so was her car. With no other options, she contacted the Boise Police Department on February 17th, 2007, to report Jeremy as a missing person and her car as stolen. Despite her growing fear that something terrible had happened to Jeremy, part of her still believed he might have left of his own accord. At the very least, she hoped the search for her car might lead to Jeremy's whereabouts.

The police initially did not delve deeply into Jeremy's disappearance. However, as Kim settled back into her home, the reality of the situation began to dawn on her. Jeremy's belongings - his computer, hunting gear, clothing - were all left untouched, an eerie testament to his sudden vanishing. This realization only added to the growing list of unanswered questions.

A week after Jeremy's disappearance, his family convened with detectives in Boise. The authorities were keen to understand more about Jeremy's life - his profession, social circles, and recent activities. It was during this meeting that the connection between Genie and Jeremy, particularly Jeremy's role in her arrest and conviction, came to light. This revelation presented a potential motive for foul play. Could Genie have harbored a grudge against Jeremy?

The plot thickened when Van disclosed that Jeremy and Genie had continued to see each other, even after her conviction. This unexpected twist only added to the complexity of the case, leaving the authorities and Jeremy's family grappling with more questions than answers. The search for the truth behind Jeremy's disappearance was now more urgent than ever, as they delved into the tangled web of relationships and resentments that surrounded him.

The initial theory that Jeremy might have left voluntarily due to financial troubles was quickly dismissed by his mother, Cheryl. Despite his challenges with money management, Cheryl was adamant that Jeremy would never abandon his daughter McKenzie, especially not for financial reasons. This belief was further cemented during McKenzie's fourth birthday, a month after Jeremy's disappearance. The pain of his absence at such a significant event for his daughter solidified Cheryl's conviction that something more sinister had transpired.

The discovery of Kim's little red car, which Jeremy had last been seen driving, marked a significant breakthrough in the investigation. Found in the desolate expanse of the Bruno Desert, 100 miles south of Boise, the car was a burnt-out shell, offering no immediate clues. The remote location and the condition of the car suggested a deliberate attempt to hide or destroy evidence. It was clear to the investigators that whoever left the car there had another means of returning to civilization, indicating the involvement of at least one other individual.

Despite an extensive ground search around the car's location, no significant clues emerged to shed light on Jeremy's whereabouts. The authorities, now suspecting foul play, intensified their efforts, delving into Jeremy's phone and bank records for any leads. They uncovered that in the days following his disappearance, Jeremy's phone had been used to make numerous calls, most of which were either to his own number or were brief, aborted calls to other numbers. One call stood out - a six-minute call from a payphone at a gas station in Mountain Home. This call, coupled with an ATM withdrawal at the same location, hinted at a possible lead. However, the lack of surveillance footage at the payphone and the mysterious one-hour gap between the ATM withdrawal and the phone call only deepened the mystery.

The friend Jeremy was supposed to meet on the night he vanished reported receiving a call from Jeremy, which he missed and could not successfully return. The Boise Police Department pursued every avenue, conducting interviews and polygraph tests with those close to Jeremy, including Genie. However, the results of these tests remained undisclosed.

Genie, questioned by the police, maintained that she had not been involved with Jeremy since her release from jail. She even consented to a polygraph test, but again, the outcomes were not made public. Jeremy's friends and family, along with investigators, were left grappling with the baffling circumstances surrounding his disappearance. No one had any concrete idea of where Jeremy could be or what might have happened to him.

Cheryl, Jeremy's mother, remained steadfast in her belief that her son would never willingly start a new life without his daughter. She was convinced that someone had harmed Jeremy, leading to his disappearance. The mystery of the phone call from the Mountain Home gas station payphone and the location of the burnt car near the same area posed intriguing questions. Was someone else involved in driving the car to the remote location? Could they have been the ones using Jeremy's phone?

In a world where it seems implausible for someone to simply vanish, the case of Jeremy's disappearance stands as a haunting reminder of the mysteries that can lurk in the shadows of everyday life. The unanswered questions and the lack of closure continue to torment those who knew and loved Jeremy, leaving them to wonder about the fate that befell him on that fateful February night.

In July of 2016, nearly a decade after Jeremy's perplexing disappearance, the saga took another tragic turn. Kim George, who had moved on with her life to some extent – remarrying and welcoming another child – tragically killed herself. The circumstances surrounding her death remain shrouded in mystery, adding another layer of sorrow and unanswered questions to an already heart-wrenching story.

Delving deeper into this intricate web of events, I came across some additional, intriguing information. Genie, a key figure in this complex narrative, seems to be connected to another mysterious case – the disappearance of Aaron Barnhart. Like Jeremy, Aaron was a witness who testified against Genie. His vanishing act occurred on December 4th, 2004, when he left his home for a dinner appointment with a friend and never returned. The circumstances of Aaron's disappearance are as puzzling as they are intriguing.

Adding to the enigma, Aaron was romantically involved with a woman who was closely connected to Genie – her best friend. This connection becomes even more intriguing considering that Aaron, his girlfriend, Genie, and Jeremy had all been present at the wedding of a mutual acquaintance. The overlapping social circles and the shared history of testifying against Genie paint a complex picture, one that suggests a potential link between the disappearances of Jeremy and Aaron.

This leads to a chilling theory: could Genie have played a role in Jeremy's disappearance as a form of retribution for his testimony, which contributed to her incarceration? And if so, is it possible that Aaron's disappearance is also connected to Genie, given their shared history and his role as a witness against her?

Jeremy Bert, who was 33 years old at the time of his disappearance, is remembered for his brown hair, hazel eyes, a stature of 6'2", and a weight of less than 200 pounds. His physical characteristics, however, tell us nothing of the emotional and complex life he led, nor do they shed light on the baffling circumstances of his disappearance.

The intertwining lives of Jeremy, Aaron, Genie, and their respective social circles create a narrative that is as compelling as it is tragic. It's a story that raises more questions than it answers, leaving us to ponder the nature of relationships, the consequences of actions, and the mysteries that sometimes remain unsolved in the face of human complexity. As we delve into these interconnected lives, we are reminded of the profound impact our actions can have on others and the enduring mysteries that can arise from the depths of human interactions.

Jodi Huisentruit

The mysterious disappearance of 27-year-old Jodi Huisentruit remains a haunting chapter in the history of Mason City. On the morning of June 27, 1995, Jodi vanished without a trace from the vicinity of her downtown apartment, setting off a perplexing investigation that continues to intrigue both locals and the nation.

The day prior to her disappearance, Jodi's life seemed as normal and vibrant as ever. She participated in a golf tournament organized by the local Chamber of Commerce, a testament to her active involvement in community events. Following the tournament, she spent time at the home of her friend, John Vansice. There, they watched a videotape of a birthday celebration, an event Vansice had earlier organized in her honor, marking a moment of joy and camaraderie in Jodi's life.

Later that evening, Jodi returned to her apartment, settling into her routine. She made a phone call to a friend, a simple act reflecting the normalcy of her evening. Known for her dedication to her job, Jodi was the morning anchor for KIMT, a role that required her to wake up in the early hours. Her typical schedule had her leaving her apartment around 3 a.m., a routine she had followed diligently.

However, the morning of June 27th unfolded with alarming irregularities. By 4 a.m., Amy Kuns, a producer at KIMT, noticed Jodi's conspicuous absence. It was highly unusual for Jodi, known for her punctuality and professionalism, to miss work without prior notice. As the hours ticked by, concern grew within the KIMT team. By 7 a.m., with no word from Jodi, the station's staff reached out to the Mason City Police Department, requesting a welfare check, a decision underscored by the growing unease over her uncharacteristic disappearance.

The police response revealed a scene that hinted at a sudden and chaotic struggle. Arriving at Jodi's apartment shortly after the call, officers discovered her red Mazda Miata parked undisturbed in the lot. It was the scattered items around the car that painted a more sinister picture—a pair of red women's pumps, a bottle of hairspray, a blow dryer, earrings, and notably, a bent car key. These items, strewn haphazardly around her vehicle, suggested a struggle had occurred, a silent testament to a confrontation that possibly led to Jodi's disappearance.

This unsettling scene set in motion an investigation that has spanned decades, leaving more questions than answers in the quest to uncover what happened to Jodi Huisentruit on that fateful summer morning.

A collaborative force of investigators from the Iowa Division of Criminal Investigation and the Federal Bureau of Investigation joined the local police in a desperate search for answers. The investigation was extensive, encompassing Jodi's apartment, the surrounding parking lot, and the nearby Winnebago River, an area that became a focal point in the early stages of the search.

Mason City's Police Chief at the time, Jack Schlieper, expressed early concerns about the nature of Jodi's disappearance, hinting at the possibility of foul play, a suspicion that cast a grim shadow over the investigation. By Wednesday, as Jodi's workplace felt the absence of their beloved news anchor, the search operation was in full swing. Schlieper, addressing the media, outlined the ongoing efforts, highlighting the involvement of police and K-9 units in combing a two-mile stretch of the Winnebago River, which meanders through a park close to Jodi's apartment on North Kentucky Avenue.

During these exhaustive searches, items of clothing were found along the riverbanks, adding another layer of mystery to the case. However, it remained unclear whether these belonged to Jodi. In a significant move, investigators impounded Jodi's Mazda Miata. From the vehicle, they managed to lift an unidentified palm print, a clue that suggested a physical struggle might have taken place near or inside the car.

Adding to the complexity of the case, police learned from some residents about unusual noises they heard on the morning of Jodi's disappearance. These sounds, initially described as resembling an animal's cries, were later theorized to be Jodi's screams, possibly indicating a violent altercation in the parking lot. This theory seemed to gain further credibility with the discovery of heel marks in the dirt on the pavement, suggesting a struggle near her car.

Eyewitness accounts also brought forward the presence of a white van in the parking lot that night, its parking lights eerily aglow. This detail added another mysterious element to the already baffling case.

Controversy arose regarding the handling of the crime scene. A friend of Jodi's raised concerns that the police did not immediately secure the area, potentially leading to evidence being contaminated or overlooked. Furthermore, Jodi's car, a potentially crucial piece of evidence, was released to her parents shortly after her disappearance, a decision that later came under scrutiny.

Jeff Brinkley, the current Chief of Police and the fourth to oversee Jodi's case, reflected on these decisions during a "48 Hours" interview. When questioned about the prompt release of the car, Brinkley acknowledged the possibility of haste in this decision. With the car no longer in police possession, he emphasized the challenges faced by the investigation, noting the team's commitment to work with the available evidence, however limited.

The enigma surrounding Jodi Huisentruit's disappearance has remained a relentless pursuit for the Mason City Police, particularly for Officer Terrance

Prochaska, who took over the case in 2010. For Prochaska, this investigation transcends the boundaries of a mere job; it has become a personal mission, consuming most of his free time. His dedication reflects not just a commitment to duty but a deep desire to unravel a mystery that has long baffled the community.

Prochaska's approach to the case is meticulous, focusing on piecing together Jodi's last known activities and uncovering the elusive details of her final hours. From her participation in a golf tournament after work to her drive home and the phone call she made to a friend, each fact forms a piece of the puzzle. However, the true challenge lies in the unknown - the gray areas and unanswered questions that linger between these established facts. What unforeseen circumstances led Jodi to oversleep that day? What prompted her hurried response to a phone call, rushing off to work? These are the gaps Prochaska aims to bridge in his quest for the truth.

Jodi's interactions at the golf tournament offer intriguing leads. She reportedly confided in friends about receiving prank calls, which had become troubling enough for her to consider involving the police and changing her phone number. This detail adds a layer of complexity to her final days, suggesting underlying concerns that may be crucial to understanding her disappearance.

John Vansice, significantly older than Jodi and the last known person to see her, remains a figure of interest in the case. In 1995, Vansice described his relationship with Jodi to KIMT in familial terms, likening her to a daughter. Despite friends of Jodi harboring suspicions about Vansice's involvement in her abduction, a different perspective is offered by LaDonna Woodford, a friend of Vansice. She recalls contacting him early on the morning of Jodi's disappearance for a walk and observes that he appeared neither anxious nor disturbed during their meeting later that day.

Although Vansice passed a polygraph test in 1995 and was never officially named a suspect, the investigation saw a significant development in March 2017. Search warrants were issued for the GPS records of vehicles associated with Vansice, a move that sparked hope for a breakthrough. Despite the high expectations, this lead ultimately proved fruitless, as nothing significant was recovered.

Chief Jeff Brinkley, in conversation with "48 Hours," reinforced the department's unwavering commitment to the case. It has remained an active investigation, never relegated to a cold case file. Brinkley's resolve is clear; he is not ready to give up on finding answers.

This sentiment is echoed by Jodi's sister, JoAnn Nathe, who also spoke with "48 Hours." While she once harbored suspicions about Vansice, Nathe emphasizes the importance of maintaining objectivity and an open mind. She acknowledges that the perpetrator could be someone entirely unexpected, a reminder of the case's enduring complexity and the need for a broad and thorough investigation.

The days leading up to Jodi Huisentruit's disappearance were marked by social engagements and outdoor activities, painting a picture of a vibrant young woman enjoying the summer. The weekend before she vanished, Jodi spent time water skiing with John Vansice and a group of friends, an excursion that was both exhilarating and reflective of her adventurous spirit.

Jodi's diary, a personal chronicle of her thoughts and experiences, provides a glimpse into this weekend. Her entry on June 25, 1995, reveals her enthusiasm: she recounts the thrill of water skiing at Coralville Reservoir near Iowa City, a place that offered both excitement and a challenge. She notes her progress in the sport, buoyed by tips from Vansice's son, Trent. This entry encapsulates a moment of joy and achievement, a stark contrast to the mystery that would soon envelop her life.

In another of her last diary entries, Jodi touches on a more contemplative note, expressing frustration with her professional life. She writes of feeling "fed up" and the challenges she faces in finding a new job. This entry sheds light on her state of mind during this period, revealing her aspirations and the uncertainties she grappled with.

Steve Ridge, a cold case investigator, delved into the details of that weekend in 2019, revealing a nuanced picture of the events. According to Ridge, while water skiing with Vansice, Jodi also had an encounter with two younger men she met that same weekend. These men, owners of a Mastercraft ski boat, invited Jodi and a female friend aboard. Ridge's investigation, informed by witness accounts from the lake that Saturday, suggests that Vansice was not particularly pleased with Jodi's decision to spend time with these younger men, though he reportedly did not display overtly negative reactions.

The time Jodi and her friend spent on the men's boat was characterized by a carefree atmosphere, with drinking and dancing on the deck. Intriguingly, Ridge notes that the boat owner captured video footage of this outing, footage that was later handed over to the Mason City police investigators.

Ridge's investigation delved into the possibility that one or both of these young men might have visited Jodi the day following their encounter or on the night she was abducted. He considered the potential for a confrontation, one that could provide insight into a motive for Jodi's abduction. Ridge's comment, "A lot of unfortunate things came together in a relatively short period of time just before Jodi went missing," encapsulates the complexity and potential significance of these interactions.

As an independent investigator, Ridge's role was crucial in shedding new light on the case. He maintained cooperation with law enforcement, ensuring that any information or leads he uncovered were shared with the authorities. His work represents a continued effort to piece together the events surrounding Jodi's disappearance, a puzzle that, despite the passage of time, continues to intrigue and challenge those who seek to solve it.

In 2011, the Globe Gazette brought to light a startling development in the Jodi Huisentruit case, reporting an explosive allegation made by Maria Ohl, a former Mason City police officer. Ohl, who had served for a decade, claimed that two of her fellow officers, Lt. Frank Stearns and Lt. Ron Vande Weerd, along with Bill Basler, a retired agent from the Iowa Division of Criminal Investigation (DCI), were involved in Jodi's abduction and murder.

Ohl stated that she first received this alarming information from an informant in 2007 and again in 2009. According to her, these informants pointed directly at the involvement of the named officers in the case. She reported these serious allegations to her superiors but claimed that her concerns were met with silence.

The situation took a dramatic turn when Ohl disclosed that she was terminated from her position, a decision she believed was directly linked to her handling of the information related to Jodi's case. She expressed deep disturbance over the matter, noting the irony of the accused officers continuing their roles funded by taxpayers, while she faced termination for acting as a whistleblower.

Adding another layer to this complex narrative, Joshua Benson, an evening anchor at an Orlando ABC affiliate and founder of FindJodi.com, mentioned that Ohl had confided in him about these allegations. However, Benson himself found no evidence to support her claims. An official investigation into the complaint also concluded without finding any validity in Ohl's allegations.

In a bizarre and unsettling incident on New Year's Eve 2020, a billboard featuring Jodi Huisentruit in Mason City was defaced by vandals. This billboard, one of three in the city displaying Jodi's image and a message imploring public assistance, was targeted in a cryptic act of vandalism. The vandals spray-painted the words "Frank Stearns Machine Shed" in bright yellow paint across the bottom half of the billboard, a message that seemed to allude to Frank Stearns, the longtime detective who had worked diligently on Jodi's case and who now serves as a city death-scene investigator.

Steve Ridge, a key figure in the ongoing investigation, provided a detailed account of the vandalism. According to Ridge, two individuals, dressed in black and acting under the cover of darkness, parked behind a tattoo parlor and used an aluminum ladder to access the billboard around 11:30 p.m. on December 31, 2019. While one held the ladder steady, the other executed the act of vandalism, spray-painting the cryptic message. Notably, the nearby bar's parking lot was full, and numerous cars passed under the billboard during the act, yet the vandals remained undetected.

Ridge later visited Frank Stearns at his rural residence on January 3, 2020. Stearns' property does include a detached building, but he lived elsewhere in 1995. The act of vandalism, seemingly intended to resurrect old wounds and accusations, did little to diminish the community's respect for Stearns. He expressed a hope that those responsible would be identified and face consequences for their actions, reflecting a continued commitment to justice and integrity in the face of such baseless and disruptive allegations.

In 2023, the ongoing mystery of Jodi Huisentruit's disappearance took a new turn with the revelation from Steve Ridge, a determined investigator in the case. Ridge brought to light the existence of a previously unknown individual in Jodi's life, a "mystery man" whom Jodi had met a mere 10 days before her abrupt vanishing. This revelation added a new, intriguing layer to the already complex case.

The relationship between Jodi and this enigmatic figure was described as unusually rapid and intense. Within the brief span of just over a week, Jodi and the "mystery man" reportedly met as many as eight times, suggesting a connection that swiftly deepened. This sudden and passionate bonding raised questions about the nature of their relationship and its potential impact on Jodi's life and safety.

Ridge's revelation about this "fast friends" relationship hinted at a scenario where such an intense and sudden connection could have triggered feelings of jealousy or resentment among others in Jodi's circle. This theory suggests that the rapid development of this relationship might have been a catalyst for events leading to Jodi's disappearance, potentially causing rifts or conflicts that had previously gone unnoticed.

This new information about the "mystery man" opened up fresh avenues of investigation and speculation. It prompted a re-examination of Jodi's interactions and relationships in the days leading up to her disappearance, with a particular focus on the potential implications of this newfound connection. The revelation by Ridge underscored the complexity of human relationships and their sometimes unforeseen consequences, particularly in a case as perplexing and tragic as that of Jodi Huisentruit.

As investigators and those following the case pondered this new development, it underscored the ongoing challenge in solving a case that had long remained shrouded in mystery. The emergence of the "mystery man" in the narrative of Jodi's life not only reignited public interest in the case but also brought new hope that this piece of the puzzle could bring them closer to understanding what happened to Jodi Huisentruit.

Kayla Berg

K ayla Berg's life story unfolds like a rich tapestry, woven with the threads of joy, struggle, and resilience. Born on the sunny day of August 29, 1993, in the picturesque town of Antigo, Wisconsin, Kayla entered the world as the beloved daughter of Hope Sprenger and James Spanbauer. Her childhood, shared with her older brother Jimmy, was a vibrant mosaic of close-knit family bonds and an unquenchable thirst for outdoor escapades. The lush green landscapes of Wisconsin provided the perfect backdrop for their family camping adventures, igniting in young Kayla a lifelong love for nature and exploration.

However, life's unpredictable currents soon brought waves of change to Kayla's early years. While she was still toddling around, her parents decided to go their separate ways. This period of transition was further complicated when her father, James, was dealt a harsh blow by fate - a diagnosis of cancer. The illness necessitated grueling dialysis treatments, and James found solace and support in moving back with Kayla's grandparents. Despite the physical distance and the complexities of their parents' separation, Kayla and her brother Jimmy maintained a strong bond with their father. Their mother, Hope, upheld a sense of unity and encouraged the siblings to visit James every other weekend, fostering an environment where love transcended the challenges of separation.

The impact of her father's illness on Kayla was profound and far-reaching. James was not just a parent to her; he was a beacon of strength and joy.

Witnessing his battle with cancer, Kayla developed a deep-seated empathy and a nurturing spirit. She became the person who could be counted on to uplift others, a friend who would go to great lengths to spread happiness and offer support in times of need.

Amidst these personal challenges, Kayla discovered a passion that would define much of her youth - gymnastics. With an innate talent for tumbling, she embraced the sport with zeal from a young age. Kayla's dedication and skill were evident in every leap and somersault, and she quickly became a star on her high school gymnastics team. Her presence at practice was like a burst of sunshine, energizing her teammates and infusing each session with her infectious enthusiasm.

As Kayla ventured into her teenage years, new horizons beckoned. In 2007, her friend introduced her to a different world - the lively party scene in Wausau, Wisconsin. Just a stone's throw from Antigo, Wausau's vibrant parties became a thrilling escape for Kayla and her friends. These weekend gatherings, brimming with youthful energy and often veiled in secrecy due to underage drinking, became a staple of their adolescent adventures. The excitement of these parties was irresistible, but it also meant navigating the complexities of teenage life, often requiring the girls to be less than truthful with their parents to partake in these nocturnal festivities.

Kayla's journey, marked by personal trials, family love, athletic prowess, and the joys and pitfalls of growing up, paints a picture of a young woman navigating the ebbs and flows of life with grace and resilience. Her story is a testament to the enduring spirit of youth, the strength of family bonds, and the unyielding power of hope.

The sophomore year of high school often marks a time of personal growth and exploration, and for Kayla Berg, it was no different. It was during this transformative period that she began a relationship with Miguel Marrero, a man four years her senior. Miguel and his friends, residents of Wausau, were the architects of the very parties that had become a cornerstone of Kayla's social life. However, this new relationship soon became a point of contention within her family. Hope, Kayla's mother, harbored deep reservations about the age difference between Kayla and Miguel and was increasingly concerned about the wild nature of the parties they attended. In a bid to steer her daughter away from what she perceived as a potentially harmful path, Hope urged Kayla to end the relationship with Miguel.

June 2009 brought about a significant shift in Kayla's life. Having just completed her sophomore year, a time when the threads of her life seemed to be entwining in complex patterns, Kayla faced a major upheaval. Hope, struggling to find stable employment and worried about Kayla's recent penchant for risk-taking and truancy, decided it was time for a change of scenery. They packed their bags and set off for Texas, leaving behind the familiarity of Antigo. This decision was not taken lightly, especially since Jimmy, Kayla's brother, had just graduated from high school and chose to stay behind, tethered to his own burgeoning life in their hometown.

The move to Texas was steeped in Hope's aspirations for a better future, a fresh start that she hoped would offer new opportunities and steer Kayla onto a safer path. But reality often has a way of diverging from our expectations. After several weeks in Texas, Hope's dreams of a brighter future began to dim under the harsh light of challenging job prospects and the stark realization that this new environment might not be the haven she had envisioned. Meanwhile, back in Wisconsin, James' health was in decline, adding another layer of concern to their already complicated situation. To add to Kayla's growing sense of displacement, her new high school in Texas lacked a gymnastics team, an absence that left a void in her life, stripping her of an activity that had not only been a source of joy but also a cornerstone of her identity.

Faced with these mounting challenges, Hope made the difficult decision to return to Antigo. On August 2, 2009, she and Kayla embarked on the journey back to their roots. However, this return was not a simple reset.

The transition period was marked by a temporary separation; while Hope stayed with a friend, Kayla moved in with her father and grandparents. This arrangement, though born out of necessity, was a poignant reminder of the fragmented nature of their lives at that moment. The separation, even within the same town, symbolized the tumultuous period they were navigating – a time of readjustment, reevaluation, and the continuous search for stability and happiness.

The narrative of Kayla Berg's life took a dramatic and mysterious turn in the early days of August 2009, a period that would later be scrutinized and replayed in the minds of those who knew her. On August 9, Kayla, ever the social butterfly, informed her mother, Hope, that she was planning to spend the night at her friend Natasha's house. The two girls, brimming with the energy and spontaneity of youth, decided to join some boys at a local party – a common enough occurrence for teenagers seeking fun and camaraderie.

However, as the dawn of August 10 crept in, an unsettling silence took hold. Natasha's mother, waking to find the girls hadn't returned, was gripped by a sense of unease. In an attempt to quell her worries, she reached out to Hope. The mothers, after discussing the situation, initially brushed off their concerns, speculating that the girls had likely ventured off to a party in Wausau and simply forgotten to check in. This theory, though plausible, soon gave way to a gnawing anxiety as the day wore on without any word from Kayla or Natasha.

Their worry intensifying, the two women decided to take action. They approached the police station, hearts heavy with concern, to report their daughters as missing. In a twist of fate that brought a momentary sigh of relief, they received news while at the station: Kayla and Natasha had been safe in town all along. This revelation, however, was just the calm before the storm.

On August 11, a new day dawned with a call from Kayla to her mother. In a casual tone, she updated Hope on her plans: she intended to spend the day with Natasha. The girls' day unfolded in a typical teenage fashion – they hung out at the local park, basking in the summer sun, and later retreated to Natasha's house. There, they were joined by Natasha's older brother and Jimmy, Kayla's own brother, in what seemed like an ordinary gathering of friends.

As the afternoon waned, around 5:00 pm, the dynamics shifted. Natasha had to leave for work, and Kayla chose to stay behind, seizing the opportunity to catch up with one of Jimmy's friends, 24-year-old Kevin Kielcheski. Their conversation flowed effortlessly, leading to a plan to meet up later that evening.

The clock marked 8:45 pm when Kevin arrived at Kayla's grandparents' house to pick her up. Little did anyone know, this ordinary evening was about to etch itself into the annals of mystery and concern, as the subsequent events would leave unanswered questions and a community in search of truth.

As the sun rose on August 12, 2009, an unsettling realization dawned upon James, Kayla's father. The absence of his daughter, who had not returned home, hung heavily in the air, prompting him to seek answers. His first point of contact was Kevin Kielcheski, the last known person to be with Kayla. Kevin's response, however, only deepened the mystery. He claimed to have dropped Kayla off at a friend's house, a statement that would soon become a critical piece in the perplexing puzzle of Kayla's whereabouts.

By August 13, the tendrils of worry had firmly wrapped themselves around Hope, Kayla's mother. Two days had passed without a word from her daughter, an unusual and alarming occurrence. Scouring her phone for any missed communications, Hope discovered a call from James the day before. The conversation that followed left her both upset and perplexed. Kayla had not returned home, a fact that disturbed Hope, yet she couldn't help but recall the recent incident where Kayla had stayed out without notice. Clinging to the hope that history was repeating itself, she anticipated a forthcoming call from her daughter.

Hope's attempts to contact Kevin proved futile. In a desperate bid for clues, she reached out to Kayla's friends on August 14. One of Kayla's gymnastics teammates provided a crucial piece of information. She recounted seeing Kayla and Kevin at McDonald's around 9:30 pm on August 11. Kayla had mentioned plans to smoke marijuana with Kevin and drive around, promising to call later that night – a call that never came.

Panic began to set in for Hope. A conversation with her son Jimmy momentarily eased her fears, as he believed Kayla was staying with a friend who had not yet been contacted. However, this brief respite was shattered on August 15. Hope learned that Jimmy had been misinformed about Kayla's location. Adding to the confusion, Kevin sent a text to Hope, stating he had dropped Kayla off at Miguel's house in Wausau. His lack of specific details, such as Kayla's attire or the exact location where he left her, only compounded the growing anxiety.

When Hope reached out to Miguel, he delivered a startling revelation: Kayla had not been to his house on the night of August 11. In fact, he hadn't seen her in over a week. This new information left Hope reeling and with no further leads to pursue.

On August 17, after days filled with worry and uncertainty, Hope made the difficult decision to report her daughter as missing. The police, considering the circumstances, listed Kayla as a potential runaway. This designation, while common in cases of missing teenagers, did little to ease the mounting concern for Kayla's safety and whereabouts. As the days passed, the mystery of what happened to Kayla Berg continued to loom large, casting a shadow of worry and speculation over the community and her loved ones.

The investigation into Kayla Berg's mysterious disappearance swiftly unfolded, with the police employing all their resources and expertise. The initial phase of the investigation focused on interviewing those closest to Kayla, starting with friends and family, as they sought to piece together the events leading up to her vanishing.

Kevin, the last known person to have seen Kayla, was among the first to be interviewed. He reiterated the story he had previously told both James and Hope – that he had dropped Kayla off at Miguel's house around 10:30 pm on the night she disappeared. He described the scene vividly: the house was dark, giving the impression that no one was home. Crucially, he noted that he hadn't actually witnessed Kayla entering the house.

As the investigation deepened, a puzzling detail emerged. The house where Kevin claimed to have dropped off Kayla was, in fact, deemed uninhabitable, with Miguel living elsewhere due to necessary repairs. This revelation was particularly striking as Kayla was reportedly aware of Miguel's temporary relocation. The investigators found it perplexing that no one else had been privy to Kayla's plans that night, leading them to speculate that she might have been concealing something from her loved ones.

The police then turned their attention to Miguel. He confirmed he had seen Kayla the Friday before her disappearance but adamantly denied seeing her on August 11. A thorough search of both his rental home and the condemned house yielded no evidence of Kayla's presence or any indication that she had been in hiding there.

As more details came to light, the police began to question the initial classification of Kayla as a runaway. Her history did not suggest a tendency to run away, and her consistent communication with her parents made her sudden silence all the more out of character. After three days, her status was updated to that of an endangered missing child, a shift that reflected the growing seriousness and urgency of the situation.

Hope, driven by a mother's determination, reached out to local news outlets, hoping to amplify the search for her daughter. Her efforts culminated in widespread media coverage, drawing the community's attention to Kayla's disappearance.

On August 26, 2009, the investigation took a hopeful turn when the police released photos based on a credible sighting of Kayla. Surveillance footage from a local Wal-Mart showed a girl, resembling Kayla, exiting a Ford Taurus and later departing in a black pickup truck. This lead, however, soon evaporated when Hope, upon reviewing the footage, concluded that the girl in the video was not her daughter.

As days turned into weeks with no sign of Kayla, the community began to buzz with rumors and theories about what could have happened to her. Each rumor, no matter how unfounded or sensational, added to the distress and heartache of her friends and family. The absence of concrete evidence or leads only fueled the speculation, leaving those who cared for Kayla in a state of agonizing uncertainty and despair.

The search for Kayla Berg transformed into a massive, multi-faceted operation, engaging various branches of law enforcement in a tireless quest for answers. In a thorough attempt to trace Kayla's steps, investigators conducted an extensive search across the road from the house where she was allegedly dropped off by Kevin. This location, situated across from the Colonial Manor Nursing Home and near a serene lake, became a focal point of the investigation. Dive teams and search dogs were deployed, with the dogs showing particular interest near a pond in the vicinity. Despite their trained instincts and the dive teams' meticulous efforts, no tangible evidence emerged from these searches.

The police, in their pursuit of clarity, focused on scrutinizing Kevin's account of the events on the night of Kayla's disappearance. Kevin maintained that he had driven straight home to Deerbrook, Wisconsin, after dropping off Kayla. This statement was corroborated by his mother, who recalled seeing her son around midnight that night. As the investigation intensified and the spotlight on him grew brighter, Kevin, sensing the mounting pressure, took the precaution of hiring a lawyer.

On October 26, 2009, the case took a significant turn when Kevin was charged with second-degree reckless endangerment. This charge was specifically related to his actions on the night Kayla vanished, notably the allegation of smoking marijuana while driving. Kevin entered a plea of not guilty, and after a protracted legal battle, the charges were dismissed on August 8, 2011, by a judge citing insufficient evidence.

In their relentless pursuit of clues, the police also examined Miguel's and Kevin's cars for any forensic evidence. Although certain spots were identified in both vehicles, subsequent tests yielded negative results. The nature of these spots remains a topic shrouded in secrecy due to the ongoing nature of the investigation. In a notable development, cadaver dogs were brought in to examine the cars in December 2009, prior to their release back to the owners. Intriguingly, the dogs singled out Kevin's car, though there was no definitive proof linking the scent they detected to Kayla's disappearance.

The investigation then shifted to analyzing cellphone records of those in Kayla's circle. Kevin's phone records confirmed communication between him and Kayla before he picked her up. However, his phone was either switched off or ran out of battery after 9:00 pm, and it remained unused until 2:00 pm the following day.

While Miguel's phone records generally supported his version of events, a striking discovery was made: an old cellphone belonging to Miguel had pinged off a tower in Lincoln County, approximately 40 miles north of Wausau, on the night Kayla disappeared. Two calls were made from this phone, but searches near the cellphone towers yielded no clues. The police, intrigued by this new information, sought to re-interview Miguel. However, he declined their request, expressing his frustration at feeling harassed by both the police and

Kayla's family.

In a continued effort to uncover any trace of Kayla, the police enlisted the National Guard on March 29, 2010. They conducted flyovers of key areas using thermal imaging technology, but these efforts, too, failed to reveal any abnormalities.

The scope of the investigation widened as police explored the possibility of human trafficking connections in Mexico and scrutinized known sex offenders in Wisconsin and surrounding states. Despite these extensive efforts, the trail remained cold.

Over the course of the investigation, cadaver and search dogs were deployed more than a dozen times, meticulously combing through woods, fields, and various sites of interest. On two separate occasions, these trained dogs indicated potential findings at properties linked to Kevin - his parents' property and the farm where he was employed. Despite these promising leads, the search teams were unable to find sufficient evidence to directly connect either location to Kayla's disappearance.

In an effort to galvanize public assistance, the FBI announced a substantial reward of $20,000 for information leading to the arrest and conviction of anyone involved in Kayla's disappearance. This move underscored the seriousness of the case and the commitment of federal authorities to solving this perplexing mystery.

Kevin, a key figure in the investigation, declined to undergo a polygraph test administered by the FBI. Instead, he opted for a test conducted by a private firm, which he claimed to have passed. Details about the test, including the specific questions asked, remain undisclosed to the public, adding another layer of intrigue to his involvement in the case.

The National Center for Missing and Exploited Children played a pivotal role in raising awareness, distributing flyers featuring an age-progressed image of Kayla. This initiative led to a significant lead from Louisville, Kentucky. A woman reported her daughter-in-law, a waitress who closely resembled the age-progressed photo and had a questionable background, as a possible match for Kayla. However, this hopeful lead ultimately resulted in a dead end as the woman was confirmed not to be the missing girl.

Tips poured in from across the United States, each one followed diligently by the police. Reports varied widely, from sightings of Kayla working at a gas station in Texas to rumors of her hiding out in Boston, Massachusetts. Yet, none of these leads brought investigators any closer to finding Kayla.

The case took a dramatic turn on October 8, 2016, with the emergence of a disturbing YouTube video dated October 2009. The video, which went viral in 2016, depicted a male subject with a girl tied up in his basement, eerily resembling Kayla. The Antigo Police Department received the video, and the FBI joined the investigation to trace its origins. The video's sudden virality led to a flood of tips, but just three days later, the video was debunked as a cruel hoax, perpetrated by actors unaware of Kayla's case.

In a poignant display of commitment to keeping Kayla's case in the public eye, Karl's Transport unveiled a trailer in 2017 adorned with Kayla's image and information. The trailer was set to travel across the United States, serving as a mobile billboard to aid in the search.

Throughout this enduring quest for answers, law enforcement officials have remained steadfast in their commitment to finding Kayla. While Miguel continues to be a person of interest, Kevin, despite never being charged or officially named a suspect, has reportedly ceased cooperating with the investigation. To date, no evidence of foul play has been uncovered, leaving investigators with few clues to pursue.

As the years pass, the possibility of Kayla being alive dwindles, a reality acknowledged by investigators with heavy hearts. Yet, despite the slim odds, their resolve to uncover the truth about Kayla Berg's fate remains unshaken.

The enigmatic disappearance of Kayla Berg has given rise to several theories, each reflecting the complexities and unanswered questions surrounding the case. These theories, born out of circumstantial evidence, varying testimonies, and the persistent efforts of those seeking the truth, continue to fuel discussions and investigations.

A predominant theory centers on Kevin's potential involvement in Kayla's disappearance. Skepticism about his narrative has been a focal point for many. Critics of his account argue that Kayla could have easily contacted Miguel directly for a ride to Wausau, casting doubt on the necessity of Kevin's involvement that evening. Adding to the suspicion are the hits by cadaver dogs on properties associated with Kevin, coupled with what some perceive as inconsistencies in his story. His reluctance to further cooperate with the investigation has only intensified the scrutiny and speculation about his role in the events of that fateful night.

Another theory posits that Kayla might have been abducted by a stranger. This possibility, though considered, is viewed with skepticism by both her mother and the police. The law enforcement perspective leans towards the belief that someone familiar with Kayla was responsible for her disappearance, potentially leading to her murder and the concealment of her body.

A third theory implicates Miguel in Kayla's disappearance. This suspicion is partly fueled by his refusal to re-engage with the police and the intriguing cellphone pings in Lincoln County, which suggest his presence in an unexpected location on the night Kayla went missing. However, those close to Kayla, including her friends, express doubts about this theory. They recall the positive nature of Miguel's relationship with Kayla and note that the couple was in the process of repairing their relationship, casting doubt on the likelihood of his involvement in any harm coming to her.

The aftermath of Kayla's disappearance has had a profound and lasting impact on those close to her. In 2011, Kayla's father passed away, holding onto the hope that his daughter would one day return. Hope, Kayla's mother, continues to believe in the possibility of her daughter being alive and eventually found.

In a touching tribute, Kayla's high school classmates honored her memory by wearing bracelets at their graduation ceremony. Each year, on the anniversary of her disappearance, Kayla's loved ones engage in a poignant ritual of releasing balloons printed with her name and containing inserts with her information, a symbol of their enduring hope and remembrance.

Susan Walsh

Susan Young's life, a tapestry of tribulations and triumphs, began on February 18th, 1960, in the northern realms of New Jersey. Her early years, shrouded in a veil of mystery, are known to few. Yet, those who hold fragments of her childhood memories paint a picture far from idyllic. Whispered stories and unconfirmed accounts suggest a youth marred by adversity – a broken home, financial struggles, and heart-wrenching tales of abuse. The enigmatic nature of Susan's upbringing only adds to the complexity of her character.

Nutley, New Jersey, a township nestled in Essex County, became the corner-stone of Susan's adult life. With its close proximity to New York City, Nutley was more than a home; it was a gateway to dreams for many of its nearly 29,000 residents. For Susan, it represented a blend of suburban tranquility and urban accessibility, a balance she navigated throughout her life.

Despite the scarcity of information about her childhood, one beacon of light shines through: her father, Floyd Merchant. His unwavering support was a rare constant in a life otherwise marked by instability. However, not all battles could be fought by a father's love. Susan's journey was fraught with personal demons – the allure of drugs and alcohol provided a temporary escape from her chaotic world, but soon became masters of her fate.

Yet, Susan's story is not one of unending despair. Within her, a fiery passion for writing and dance burned brightly. These creative outlets offered her a sanctuary, a realm where she could channel her tumultuous emotions and experiences into art. Her poetry became a canvas for her soul, while her graceful movements in dance were a physical manifestation of her inner turmoil and resilience.

Her beauty, both internal and external, did not go unnoticed. Susan's allure captivated many, yet her aspirations soared beyond the confines of her challenging upbringing. She dreamt of a glamorous life, a successful career in writing, and a home that overlooked the verdant expanse of Central Park – a stark contrast to the realities she faced.

As she navigated her late teens and early twenties, the vibrant music scene of the 1980s became both a haven and a hazard. The nightlife's seductive blend of rhythm and vice made her battle with substance abuse all the more challenging. Yet, Susan was determined to carve her own path. After graduating from high school, she enrolled at William Paterson University. Balancing academia with financial realities, she took a job at Show World Center in Times Square, a world far removed from the academic halls she frequented by day.

This duality of life – student by day, dancer by night – was a testament to Susan's resilience and determination. Yet, it was also a portal to a world that was difficult to escape. Despite the challenges, her spirit remained unbroken. She found solace in journalism, joining the staff of her college newspaper, The Beacon, and nurturing her love for writing.

Susan's life was a journey of soaring highs and profound lows. Her battle with addiction, her marriage to Mark Walsh, and her struggles as a single mother after their separation painted a portrait of a woman constantly fighting against the odds. Through it all, she remained committed to her son David, her writing, and her dreams.

Her journey from the shadowed stages of Show World to the esteemed halls of William Paterson University, and her transition from a life of adversity to one of aspiration, is a narrative of resilience. Susan Young's life story, with all its complexities and contradictions, stands as a testament to the indomitable human spirit, an unyielding pursuit of dreams amidst life's relentless challenges.

Susan Young's life was deeply intertwined with her unwavering commitment to her son, who was always her top priority. Friends and colleagues often spoke of her exceptional dedication as a mother, emphasizing how she devoted every possible moment to nurturing and caring for him. This profound maternal love was a constant source of strength and motivation throughout her challenging journey.

In 1994, when Susan was 34, a significant opportunity arose. She connected with James Ridgeway, a writer for the Village Voice, who was working on a book about the sex industry. Susan eagerly joined this project, seeing it as a chance to advance her career in journalism. Their first major collaboration was an article for the Village Voice in August 1994, exposing the exploitation of Russian dancers in the United States. This assignment required Susan to delve back into the murky world of sex work, a realm she had once left behind.

Over the next two years, Susan played a crucial role in Ridgeway's research, going undercover in strip clubs and gathering valuable information. While she was officially credited as a research associate in Ridgeway's book 'Red Light', this period also marked her gradual re-immersion into the world of exotic dancing, a move that would have significant consequences.

In 1995, Susan embarked on a unique assignment for The Voice, investigating an underground vampire culture in New York City. She immersed herself in this subculture, uncovering a community seeking escapism through fantasy, much like her own life's dichotomy. However, despite her thorough investigation, her article was ultimately not published by The Voice, dealing a significant blow to her aspirations.

Faced with the challenges of the journalism industry, Susan gradually found herself returning to exotic dancing. This shift marked a concerning turn in her life, as she began to lose control over the very world she sought to use for her benefit.

By 1996, Susan's life had become increasingly complex. Her long-standing sobriety began to waver, and her personal life grew more complicated due to her relationships with men she met through her work. These relationships often led to possessiveness and stalking, adding to the myriad of challenges she faced.

During this period, Christian Peppo, a younger man who had become a significant part of her life, provided support and care for her son. Their relationship, beneficial in some respects, also led to jealousy and conflict with others who were drawn to Susan.

The challenges Susan was facing became evident at the book launch party for Ridgeway's 'Red Light' in June 1996. Her struggle with substance abuse, her expressed fears for her safety, and signs of self-harm were clear indicators of the turmoil she was experiencing.

On July 16th, 1996, amidst the oppressive heat of Nutley, Susan made a mysterious phone call after arranging for her son's care with her ex-husband. The content and purpose of this call remain unknown, adding to the enigmatic narrative of Susan Young's life.

Susan's life had taken a dramatic turn in 1994 when she teamed up with James Ridgeway, a writer for the Village Voice, to expose the exploitation of Russian dancers in the United States. This project led her back into the world of sex work, a realm she had once left behind. Her dedication to journalism and the pursuit of a better life for herself and her son was evident in her willingness to delve into this murky world.

However, by 1996, Susan's life had become increasingly complex. Her sobriety wavered, and she found herself entangled in relationships with men she met through her work. These relationships often turned possessive and even stalking. Christian Peppo, a significant figure in her life during this period, provided support and care for her son, but their relationship had its challenges.

On July 16th, 1996, Susan made a mysterious phone call, the nature of which remains unknown. She mentioned needing to call her manager, the man who booked her in clubs. However, her friends, including Melissa, suspected there might have been an ulterior motive for this call. Some believed that Susan's manager may have played a role in selling her drugs.

Later that day, Susan's friend Melissa became concerned when Susan didn't return her calls. She decided to check on her at Susan's apartment. Melissa was greeted by locked doors and closed windows, a departure from Susan's usual habit of leaving doors open and windows ajar in the sweltering summer heat. Despite her discomfort, Melissa left, planning to return later.

Approximately an hour later, Melissa returned to find no response from Susan. Mark, Susan's ex-husband, and David, her son, arrived, but they hadn't seen her since around noon. The worry escalated, and Melissa continued paging Susan throughout the day and night.

Around 6:00 p.m., Joey, another friend of Susan's, arrived at her place to give her a ride to work. However, Susan was nowhere to be found, and Joey left after waiting for her. This raised concerns, but no one could pinpoint Susan's whereabouts.

After 24 hours had passed, Mark contacted the Nutley Police Department to report Susan missing. The police interviewed Mark and David and gained access to Susan's apartment, where they found her personal belongings on the kitchen table. There were no signs of a struggle or foul play, suggesting that Susan may have left willingly.

Authorities started considering the possibility of foul play, and they began gathering information about the people in Susan's life. Two individuals initially drew their attention: Christian Peppo and Mark Walsh. Both were considered possible suspects, but there was little evidence implicating either of them.

As weeks turned into months, police received various tips and sightings of Susan, but none led to her whereabouts. The media picked up Susan's story, and tips poured in, often suggesting that she was living on the streets, struggling with addiction, and engaging in risky behavior.

Susan's friends and family believed that she would never willingly abandon her son, but the trail grew colder with time. Some speculated that Susan had been targeted due to her involvement in the world of sex work and her investigative journalism. Rumors circulated, from the Russian mafia to an underground vampire club, but none could be substantiated.

One year after Susan's disappearance, authorities concluded that she might have fallen back into addiction and been preyed upon by dangerous indi-viduals. It was a heartbreaking scenario, leaving many frustrated with the investigation's progress.

Years passed without significant developments in Susan's case, and it wasn't until 2005 that there was any movement. During this time, her friends and family continued to hold onto hope, while authorities grappled with the complexities of her disappearance. The mystery of Susan Young's vanishing act remained unsolved, leaving behind a trail of questions and a haunting sense of loss.

Lieutenant Steve Rogers had a mission as the lieutenant commander of the Nutley Police Department: to reopen cold cases and breathe new life into old mysteries. The first case on his list was Susan's, and he embarked on this reinvigorated investigation with the hope of uncovering fresh leads and answers that had eluded them for years.

As Rogers delved into the case, he revisited the evidence, reinterviewed friends and family, and brought a renewed focus to Susan's disappearance. It was during this process that he stumbled upon a critical discovery that had previously been overlooked—an item of significance hidden within the evidence.

Among the items collected from Susan's apartment and logged into evidence was her calendar. Susan was known for her meticulous record-keeping, and her calendar was a treasure trove of information. Strangely, one page was missing from her calendar, the page corresponding to July 1996—the very month she disappeared. This missing page raised suspicions for Rogers.

He believed that this page might have contained crucial information that the suspect wanted to conceal. It could have held names, locations, or other details that investigators could have used to track down the person responsible for Susan's disappearance. It was a baffling discovery, leaving Rogers wondering why the perpetrator hadn't simply taken the entire calendar.

Rogers was determined to revisit the scene of the disappearance, Susan's apartment. However, when he arrived, he found that Mark, Susan's ex-husband who still lived there, was not open to conversations or allowing further investigation on the premises. Instead, Mark's attorney requested that any communication with his client be conducted through his office, which added another layer of complexity to the case.

Despite Mark's reluctance to cooperate further, Rogers didn't consider this as evidence of guilt. It was more likely that Mark wished to leave the past behind and avoid reopening old wounds. Over the years, Susan's case had transformed from a local sensation to a niche mystery, fading from the spotlight.

However, the investigation continued, and in a 2006 interview, Lieutenant Commander Rogers hinted at a new piece of evidence that pointed toward a homicide. The nature of this evidence was kept confidential to protect the integrity of the case. It was a glimmer of hope for those still seeking answers, indicating that Susan's case might not be forgotten.

In 2006, more than ten years after Susan's disappearance, investigators discussed using sonar technology to search for her body in a reservoir near Montclair, just four miles from Nutley. This reservoir held significance as Susan had often walked there to clear her mind. Coincidentally, it was also close to a property owned by Mark Walsh's father. However, the results of this search have not been revealed.

Over two decades have passed since Susan Young vanished, leaving behind a trail of unanswered questions and a sense of loss that lingers. Several theories have circulated regarding her disappearance. Some believe she may have chosen to leave her life behind due to addiction and personal struggles, while others suspect her work as a journalist may have made her a target. Additionally, there are theories that someone close to her could have been involved.

Despite the numerous speculations and theories, Susan's fate remains unknown. In 23 years, her son David, who was only 11 when she disappeared, has grown into adulthood. The apartment building and the streets of Nutley have witnessed changes, yet the memory of Susan and the mystery surrounding her disappearance endure.

The payphone that Susan used has become a relic in the age of cell phones, and Times Square, once a hub for various activities, has transformed into a tourist-friendly destination. However, for those who remember Susan and seek the truth about her disappearance, the passage of time has only deepened the longing for answers. Susan's story is one of enduring mystery, a story that refuses to fade into the shadows, and a story that awaits its resolution.

April Pritzer

On a crisp winter's day, February 19, 1974, Gloria Denton welcomed into the world a daughter, April Beth. Young and navigating the complexities of motherhood, Gloria faced a myriad of challenges. April's father, a stoic Vietnam veteran, added another layer to the intricate family dynamics. Gloria, with unwavering resolve, committed herself to raising April single-handedly, imbuing her journey with love and sacrifice.

Tragedy struck when April was merely three years old; Gloria, deemed too young to be a mother, heartbreakingly lost custody to relatives. Despite this separation, Gloria remained an ever-present figure in April's life. Their bond, unyielding and profound, flourished over years of heartfelt letters and shared dreams. April, with her radiant, caring personality, echoed her mother's strength and love.

April's essence was a tapestry of contrasts: a nurturing soul with an adventurous spirit. She thrived in the rugged beauty of northwestern Arkansas, embracing activities like hiking, rock climbing, and hang gliding. Clarksville, nestled between the Arkansas River and the Ozark Mountains, was her playground and sanctuary. Yet, April's interests were as diverse as her spirit; she found joy in cooking, a reflection of her nurturing heart, and in music, often singing with a passion inherited from Gloria.

As April turned 17 in 1991, she made a defining choice: to reunite with Gloria. This reunion fortified their bond, making them inseparable. They shared a vow – nothing would ever part them again.

Life's journey took unexpected turns. When Gloria moved to East Texas, April, surprisingly, chose to stay in Clarksville. This decision, a testament to her independent spirit, puzzled Gloria but was respected. Distance never dimmed their connection; they shared every triumph and trial, including a challenging episode in April's early 20s.

April's vivacious personality often drew people to her, but one fateful night, it led to a dire misstep. After a night out, she offered to drive two new acquaintances home, not fully sober.

In the whirlwind of events, April found herself at a police station, being processed for a misdemeanor DWI. Faced with the daunting prospect of fines and jail time, she was unexpectedly offered a way out: become a drug informant. It was a peculiar offer, considering her charge, but with methamphetamine found with her passengers, law enforcement saw an opportunity in April.

Reluctantly, April agreed, plunging into a shadowy world of undercover operations. She was tasked with infiltrating bars and clubs, gathering intel on a sprawling drug ring that stretched from Clarksville to Southern California. Under the guidance of a handler in Little Rock, April navigated this dangerous terrain, armed with hidden cameras and recording devices. Her efforts were instrumental in providing law enforcement with a deeper understanding of the drug network.

Throughout this risky endeavor, April kept her mother, Gloria, informed, downplaying the dangers to ease her worries. But the risks were real, and eventually, her cover was blown. With her safety compromised, law enforcement hastily extracted her from the operation, advising her to disappear without a trace.

April fled to Texas, seeking refuge with relatives in the Dallas-Fort Worth area, possibly Longview. There, she hoped to leave her past and the dangers of Arkansas behind. As she settled into her new life, April encountered Chase Spitzer, a young man whose charm and confidence instantly captivated her. Their romance blossomed rapidly, and soon, they were married. April's new life seemed idyllic, with her father-in-law gifting them a lavish house, a stark contrast to her previous struggles.

However, not everyone was thrilled about April's new chapter. Her in-laws, learning about her past as an informant, harbored reservations about the union. Despite this, Chase's devotion to April never wavered.

The couple's joy multiplied with the news of April's pregnancy. Her nurturing nature found a new outlet as she eagerly anticipated motherhood. But as she neared her due date, a knock at her door marked the return of her tumultuous past. An agent from the Drug Enforcement Agency stood there, with news that arrests had been made in the drug ring case. They needed April to return to Arkansas to testify in the trial. The timing couldn't have been worse, and April, heavily pregnant and ensconced in her new life, faced a daunting dilemma.

April stood at a crossroads, torn between her past and her new life. The DEA's ultimatum was stark: return to Arkansas to testify or face the consequences, which could include not only the DWI charge but potential involvement in the drug operation. Despite her reluctance, April found herself back in Arkansas, submerged in a high-stakes legal battle.

This unexpected return strained her relationship with her in-laws and revealed to Gloria the full extent of April's predicament. Ensconced in motels and guarded by federal officers, April's days were marked by a cloak-and-dagger existence. Her courtroom appearances were orchestrated with utmost secrecy, her identity shielded under protective gear.

The complexity of the drug trade in Arkansas, a web of operations reaching from Clarksville to Southern California, was a revelation to many. April's testimony, crucial in securing convictions of over 30 individuals, exposed the breadth of these networks, with connections spanning 1,400 miles.

Post-trial, April returned to Fort Worth, her life seemingly resuming its course with the birth of her daughter. Yet the ordeal had left an indelible mark. Paranoia crept in, a constant shadow over her life. Her fear of retribution was so intense that she resorted to using different names and avoided obtaining a Texas driver's license, leading to numerous fines.

April's second pregnancy brought a glimmer of hope, a chance to reconnect with her nurturing side. However, her growing paranoia started to strain her marriage with Chase. Their once peaceful home turned into a fortress, with extra locks, surveillance cameras, and the children sleeping in the master bedroom for safety.

This escalating fear and tension began to erode the foundation of April and Chase's relationship. Disagreements became frequent and complex, with April's unease casting a pall over their life together. Chase's love for April was unwavering, but finding a way to alleviate her fears proved increasingly challenging.

April's life took a turbulent turn as she grappled with the overwhelming challenges of her mental health, strained relationships, and the loss of her children. Turning to alcohol for comfort, her situation worsened, leading to a diagnosis of bipolar disorder. This revelation shed light on her struggles but also introduced new complexities. Disenchanted with her prescribed medications, April chose to forego them, exacerbating her insomnia and paranoia.

The turmoil in her life took a toll on her marriage to Chase. Despite their love, the couple divorced, yet couldn't fully let go of each other. Their on-again, off-again relationship, kept secret from Chase's disapproving parents, was a rollercoaster of emotions and hope. But as April's mental health deteriorated, their attempts at reconciliation faltered.

By February 2003, April, grappling with her demons, moved out with her daughters, taking up a job at a gas station convenience store. However, her life unraveled further when Child Protective Services, influenced by Chase and his family, removed her children due to concerns about her well-being and living conditions.

Amidst this chaos, April crossed paths with John Lopez, a man entangled in a web of illegal activities. Despite common misconceptions, April's relationship with Lopez was not romantic but rather a friendship, facilitated by John and his wife, Rose. They proposed a change of scenery for April, suggesting that time away might help her rebuild her life and potentially improve her chances of regaining custody of her children.

With a mix of hope and desperation, April embarked on a journey to California with the Lopezes in December 2003. She settled in San Bernardino County, an area known for its harsh desert landscape and high drug activity, far from the picturesque California many envision. Here, April faced a new set of challenges, from the unforgiving environment to her precarious association with the Lopezes.

The Lopezes' intentions soon became questionable. They sold April a Jeep, which turned out to be stolen, and left her stranded at a desert party among strangers. This abandonment marked the end of her ties with the Lopezes and the beginning of her association with Mike Bernal. Bernal offered April a place to stay on his property, a decision April accepted out of necessity.

Nestled in the Western Mojave Desert, Newberry Springs is a remote community, home to fewer than 3,000 people. In this isolated place, April found herself at the mercy of the Bernal family, her life spiraling further into despair. The situation quickly deteriorated, revealing the shady dealings on the Bernal property, including involvement in illegal activities and the drug trade. April, already vulnerable, began to succumb to the lure of drugs and alcohol.

Among those she met was Steve Wilkinson, a seemingly amiable figure with a dark past. Unbeknownst to April, Wilkinson was a key player in the drug world, having served time in federal prison for his involvement in the very drug ring she had testified against. In this precarious world, April also encountered Chuck Hollister and a mysterious figure known as "Dan Dan."

Hollister, a Vietnam veteran, was known for his generosity towards those in need, but he harbored a darker side marked by drug abuse and a volatile temper. Dan Dan, a reclusive and dangerous character, lived in old mining shacks and fiercely guarded his claim to the Red Dog mine in Ludlow. His aggressive nature and threatening writings painted a picture of a man not to be crossed.

April's life became entangled with these characters, leading her down a path fraught with danger and dependency. A violent confrontation between April, Bernal, Hollister, and Dan Dan resulted in April suffering a bullet wound to her leg. Wilkinson, despite his criminal background, tended to her injuries and assured her mother, Gloria, that she would recover.

Despite Gloria's pleas for her to return home, April remained, her situation growing increasingly dire. She became homeless and desperate, relying on the kindness of acquaintances for shelter and sustenance. Ashamed of her plight, she concealed the truth from her mother, painting a falsely rosy picture of her life in California.

In the aftermath of her tumultuous life with Bernal, the confrontation with Dan Dan and Chuck, and the harrowing gunshot incident, April reached a breaking point. One day, with her leg healed but her spirit broken, she found herself wandering aimlessly down Route 66. Lost and desperate, she was too ashamed to seek help from her mother. It was then that Mark Killebrew, a kind stranger, noticed her distress and offered assistance. He brought April to his mother, Barbara's house, where a new friendship began to blossom.

Barbara, an elderly woman who needed help moving around, found a caregiver in April. April, in turn, found solace in Barbara's company, a rare soul who cared for her without ulterior motives. Encouraged by Barbara, April finally mustered the courage to reveal the truth of her situation to her mother, Gloria. This confession was a cathartic moment for April, who had been burdened with the weight of her secrets and struggles.

Determined to start anew, April planned to move back in with her mother, who was relocating to Clarksville, Arkansas. She decided to wait until Gloria had settled before joining her, planning to travel by bus once Gloria wired her the money. However, fate had other plans.

In the interim, April stayed with Wilkinson for a time. Despite her intention to return to her family, a chance encounter with Brandi Brooks, someone she had testified against back in Arkansas, left her shaken and fearful. This meeting exposed her past as a confidential informant to those she was surrounded by, putting her in grave danger.

April's conversation with Gloria following this encounter was filled with fear and urgency. Gloria urged her to leave immediately, but April decided to wait until her mother was ready in Clarksville. In the meantime, she sought refuge with Chuck Hollister, despite their past issues. This decision would be the last Gloria would hear of her daughter's whereabouts.

After several days of unreturned calls, Gloria's concern escalated. When Barbara informed her that April had planned to return to Arkansas but hadn't arrived, alarm bells rang. Gloria's attempts to file a missing person report were initially met with skepticism from the authorities, who suggested April might have simply chosen to disappear. However, with Barbara's help, a missing person report was finally filed on July 16th.

Four days after filing the missing person report, on July 20th, Gloria received a call from Chuck Hollister. He claimed he'd been out of town, which explained his silence. Chuck's story about April's disappearance was inconsistent and puzzling. He first said he thought April had left for home, as her luggage remained, but then claimed she had gone to stay with Steve Wilkinson, known for his drug trade ties and connection to Brandi Brooks.

Detective Pennington's visit to Chuck's home yielded no new information, and Chuck even refused him entry. Another detective, Maurice Spain, also received a conflicting story from Chuck. Gloria's attempt to clarify these discrepancies was met with a dead end as Chuck had changed his phone number.

The investigation stagnated until a transit employee reported a passenger's eerie comment about knowing April's whereabouts – "in a hole." This lead took detectives to a woman who admitted hearing at a party that April was killed and hidden in a mineshaft. Given the vast number of mines in the area, the search seemed daunting.

Deputy Coroner David Van Norman enlisted Joe Pasitola, a local historian familiar with the mines, to help. Meanwhile, hundreds of miles north in Oregon, at a truck stop, a graffiti message was found related to April's disappearance. Oregon's mention resonated with Chuck's earlier claim of being there, raising suspicions.

Surveillance footage from the Oregon truck stop was obtained, revealing a man resembling Chuck. Tricia, Chuck's estranged daughter, could not confirm the man's identity but noted his resemblance to her father. This connection to Oregon, where Chuck claimed to have been, added another layer of mystery to the case.

The Sheriff's Department launched a large-scale search in the area indicated by the graffiti. Despite their efforts, the expansive terrain and numerous mineshafts made the search challenging, and no significant findings emerged.

Gloria, desperate for answers, reviewed hours of truck stop footage and observed a man resembling Chuck. This sighting, coupled with the graffiti in Oregon and Chuck's earlier alibi, seemed more than a coincidence. Yet, despite all these efforts and leads, April's whereabouts remained a mystery, leaving Gloria and the investigators grappling with more questions than answers.

Gloria, driven by a mother's relentless determination, scoured through her phone records, contacting every number April had used to reach her. The responses varied, but a haunting narrative emerged: April had been murdered and her body concealed in a mineshaft. One location repeatedly surfaced in these conversations – the mines of Ludlow, connected to Chuck Hollister's former friend, Dan Dan, who owned the Red Dog mine there.

Despite numerous visits from Detective Pennington, Dan Dan remained tight-lipped. Another twist emerged when Chuck Hollister provided varying accounts of April's last days, adding to the confusion and suspicion. Meanwhile, Steve Wilkinson, another figure in this complex web, denied April had returned to his residence after staying with Chuck.

The authorities managed to search the Red Dog mine in December 2004, but found nothing. The search was hindered by the mine's dangerous conditions, including unstable areas and rattlesnakes. As time passed, the lack of concrete leads frustrated the police, and the local rumor mill continued to churn out theories about April being hidden in a mineshaft.

Gloria relentlessly pursued every avenue, writing letters and sending flyers to Chuck Hollister, who never responded. Then, a break came in January 2005 when Andreea Pruitt, the owner of the Baghdad Cafe, recognized April as a former employee. Andrea recalled April's sudden and unexplained departure from the cafe, particularly disturbed by April's bruised appearance on her last day.

Nearly a year later, in December 2005, a significant clue was discovered by

Joe Passatola, who found discarded women's clothing, including items that Gloria had sent to April, near the Indian Queen mine. This discovery prompted Gloria to visit the area in January 2006. There, she found more clothing that she identified as April's, including the white suitcase she had sent and a black lace bra, near the Red Dog mine. However, the elements had degraded any potential forensic evidence.

During her visit, Gloria met with various people April had associated with, but none could provide insight into her disappearance. Chuck Hollister's deathbed declaration of innocence in September 2006 and Dan Dan's hospital confession to Gloria added more layers to the mystery. A woman later claimed that Dan Dan, on his deathbed, confessed to killing April, but even with this revelation, April's fate remained shrouded in mystery.

Over the ensuing years, countless searches were conducted in the mines dotting the area, involving the police, private search teams, and volunteers. Groups like Trinity Search and Rescue, the Mojave Underground, Underground Explorers, and Texas Equusearch dedicated time and resources, delving deep into the mines, sometimes reaching depths of 3,000 feet. Despite these extensive efforts, only garments that might have belonged to April were discovered, and a stone cross thought to be a memorial to Chuck Hollister, not related to April.

In 2008, a butterfly garden was inaugurated at the Desert Discovery Center in Barstow, dedicated to April's memory, keeping her story and the search alive. Despite physical challenges, Gloria herself ventured into the mines, alongside expert teams, in a relentless quest for her daughter.

Gloria's search extended beyond the mines. She spoke with people she suspected knew more than they were admitting, sometimes wearing a wire to record conversations. One person of interest who survived longer than others connected to April's disappearance was Steve Wilkinson. He was a known drug kingpin and served time for his involvement in the drug ring that April testified against. In conversations with Gloria, Wilkinson revealed disturbing details about his criminal past and his suspicions about others possibly involved in April's disappearance.

Wilkinson's arrest in 2015 on major drug charges and subsequent death in a mysterious plane crash added more layers to the saga. The crash's odd circumstances and post-death Facebook activity fueled rumors that Wilkinson might have staged his death to escape the law.

The deaths of Wilkinson, Hollister, and Dan Dan closed the chapter on the most likely suspects in April's disappearance. Gloria pondered various theories, including the possibility that April's body was moved or even taken aboard Wilkinson's ill-fated flight.

In her exhaustive search, Gloria encountered Dan Dan in the hospital, where he denied involvement but made cryptic statements about April and Brandy Brooks. A woman later claimed Dan Dan confessed to killing April, a revelation that, while unverified, haunted Gloria.

Three primary theories have emerged regarding April's fate: an unknown individual seeking revenge for the trial, Wilkinson's direct or indirect involvement, or Dan Dan's responsibility, possibly disposing of April in the mines he knew well. The truth remains elusive, shrouded in the vast expanse of the Mojave Desert and the silence of those who might have known.

April Pitzer, last seen in Newberry Springs, California, in 2004, remains a missing person. Described as a Caucasian female with brown hair and hazel eyes, standing five feet nine inches tall, weighing between 120 and 130 pounds, and with several distinctive scars, April's disappearance continues to baffle and grieve those who knew her.

Gloria Denton, transformed by her quest, remains a mother on a mission, not just seeking her daughter but also standing as a voice for those whose disappearances go unreported and mourned. She believes that every missing person, regardless of their life's choices or challenges, deserves to be found and remembered.

Brandon Swanson

orn and raised in the heartwarming small town of Marshall, the county seat of Lyon County in the quaint southwestern corner of Minnesota, Brandon Swanson's journey began with his high school graduation from Marshall High School in the year 2007. Fueled by a passion for renewable energy and a keen interest in the burgeoning field of wind technology, Brandon made the decisive choice to embark on an educational journey at Minnesota West Community and Technical College, located in the serene town of Canby. Here, he immersed himself in an intensive one-year program focused on the intricate workings of wind turbines, a field that promised a future of sustainable energy and innovation.

As the academic year at Minnesota West drew to a close on May 13, 2008, the campus was abuzz with the excitement of completion and the anticipation of new beginnings. Swanson, sharing in this collective joy, decided to spend the evening in Canby, reveling in the accomplishments of the year with his friends. In the spirit of celebration, he attended not one, but two festive gatherings, where he was seen enjoying the occasion with a few drinks. His friends, however, noted that while he partook in the merriment, he did not appear to overindulge to the point of visible intoxication.

The air of celebration, however, soon turned to an eerie mystery that would haunt the town. Swanson embarked on his 30-mile (48 km) drive back to Marshall before the stroke of midnight. It was in the early hours of the morning, just before 2 a.m., when an unexpected call jolted his parents,

Annette and Brian Swanson. On the other end was Brandon, his voice calm yet concerned, explaining that he had accidentally driven his Chevrolet Lumina off the road and into a ditch, a predicament from which he could not extricate his vehicle. Thankfully, he was unharmed, but he needed their help to get back home.

Annette and Brian, filled with parental concern and urgency, immediately set out in their pickup truck, determined to locate their son in the darkness of the night. They maintained a phone connection with Brandon, despite the challenges of occasional call hangups and signal drops. Brandon, meanwhile, stayed with his car, attempting to guide his parents to his location by intermittently flashing his car's lights. Yet, in a bewildering twist, neither he saw their signals, nor did they see his.

As the night deepened, Brandon, in a decision that would forever change the course of events, resolved to leave his car. He had spotted lights in the distance, leading him to believe he was near Lynd, a small town about 7 miles southwest of Marshall. He instructed his father to meet him at the parking lot of a local bar. Brian, with a mix of worry and hope, began driving towards the designated spot, all the while conversing with his son.

The narrative took a harrowing turn shortly after 2:30 a.m., 47 minutes into their phone conversation. In a sudden and chilling interruption, Brandon exclaimed "Oh, shit!" and then... silence. The line went dead, leaving his words hanging in the air, a haunting echo in the night. Despite desperate attempts by his parents to reconnect, to hear his voice again, Brandon vanished into the night, leaving no trace, no further word. The mystery of Brandon Swanson remains unsolved, a poignant reminder of a night that started in celebration and ended in an enigma that still lingers.

As dawn broke on that fateful day, with the first rays of sunlight barely touching the sky at 6:30 a.m., Annette and Brian Swanson, fraught with worry and desperation, made the crucial decision to report their son Brandon as missing to the local Lynd police department. Their parental instincts told them something was amiss, but their concerns were initially met with a lackluster response. The officers, perhaps accustomed to the youthful antics of college students celebrating the end of an academic year, downplayed the urgency of the situation. Annette vividly remembers one officer's words, stating that it was Brandon's "right to be missing", a statement that, while technically true, did little to ease the growing dread in the hearts of the worried parents.

As the morning sun climbed higher, casting its light over the sleepy town of Lynd, the police began to sense the gravity of the situation. A search operation was initiated, yet it yielded no clues, no trace of Brandon either within the town's boundaries or its outskirts. Recognizing the need for additional resources, the Lynd police reached out to the Lyon County Sheriff's office, led by Sheriff Joel Dahl. Determined to uncover any leads, the sheriff's office promptly obtained Brandon's cell phone records. These records shed new light on the mystery, revealing that Brandon's calls had originated not from Lynd, but from somewhere near Taunton, along State Highway 68. This route, a main artery to Canby, was located northwest of Marshall, a startling 25 miles (40 km) away from Lynd. The plot thickened as the search shifted gears, honing in on this new area of interest.

In this widened search zone, nestled along the serene and often overlooked landscapes of Lincoln County, a significant discovery was made. Deputies found Brandon's car, a Chevrolet Lumina, abandoned in a lonely ditch off a secluded gravel road, just a mile north of Highway 68. This new development brought another player into the unfolding drama – the Lincoln County Sheriff's office, headed by Sheriff Jack Vizecky.

Sheriff Vizecky shared with the media a curious detail about the state of the Lumina. It was found perched precariously on the edge of an incline, in such a position that while the car itself was not substantially damaged, its wheels were suspended, rendering it immobile. This puzzling scenario raised more questions than answers. What's more, the surrounding area, a blend of grass and gravel, offered no further clues. The lack of discernible tracks was a silent testament to the mystery of Brandon's disappearance. It left investigators and family alike grappling with an unsettling reality – there was no way to determine which direction Brandon might have ventured on foot after leaving his stranded vehicle.

As the days passed, the investigation continued, weaving through the complexities of the case, each new revelation adding layers to an already intricate mystery. The search for Brandon Swanson became not just a mission of law enforcement but a story that gripped the hearts of a community.

Each thread of information added depth to the unfolding mystery. One such vital thread was the routing of Brandon's final cellphone call through a tower strategically positioned at the crossroads of County Routes 3 and 10, near Minneota, another small town dotting the landscape along Highway 68. This piece of information, a beacon in the sea of uncertainties, came into sharper focus by May 15. Investigators, piecing together the digital breadcrumbs, determined that Brandon's call originated from within a 5-mile (8.0 km) radius of this tower. This discovery spurred a concentrated effort in the search, narrowing down the vast expanse of land to a more focused area.

This radius of mystery not only encompassed parts of Lyon County but also stretched its invisible fingers into the neighboring Yellow Medicine County to the north, thereby bringing additional authorities into the fold of this complex search operation.

Sheriff Joel Dahl, a key figure in navigating this labyrinthine case, observed a notable landmark from the area: the glaring red light atop a Taunton grain elevator, piercing the night sky. He speculated that this beacon could have misled Brandon into believing that Lynd was tantalizingly within walking distance. This theory fueled the search efforts, which were now being amplified by a coordinated approach. Ground searches were intensively conducted, complemented by an aerial team scanning from the skies. To add another layer to this multifaceted search, canine units, including search dogs from the Twin Cities, joined the fray.

In a significant development, a team of bloodhounds from nearby Codington County, South Dakota, picked up what appeared to be a scent trail of Brandon. This trail, spanning 3 miles, wove its way through the field roads in a west-northwest direction, leading to an abandoned farm, and continued along the Yellow Medicine River. The trail came to an enigmatic end at a point where it seemed to merge into the river itself.

Brandon's father vividly recalled his son mentioning passing fences and hearing the sound of water nearby during their final phone call. This detail, coupled with the bloodhounds' trail, gave rise to a harrowing theory: Brandon might have met his fate in the river. Acting on this possibility, boats from the state's Department of Natural Resources were deployed along the river, with gates installed to aid the search. In some parts of Lincoln County, the river had been a daunting 10 feet deep on the morning of Brandon's disappearance, although the water levels had since receded, as noted by Dahl.

The search operation was exhaustive. Deputies patrolled the riverbanks, while horses and all-terrain vehicles scoured the surrounding terrain. Despite the extensive efforts and the palpable urgency of the search, Sheriff Dahl, after careful consideration, decided against a more organized, extensive ground search. The decision was likely weighed down by the complexities and challenges of the terrain, as well as the elusive nature of the clues at hand.

The initial search efforts, comprehensive though they were, yielded no tangible signs of his whereabouts. The profound sense of loss and unresolved mystery weighed heavily on the community and the Swanson family. Despite the dwindling leads, Sheriff Jack Vizecky, fueled by a relentless sense of duty and hope, embarked on a solitary, poignant ritual. For 30 consecutive days, he walked the two miles (3.2 km) stretch of the Yellow Medicine River in the area, each step a testament to the unwavering resolve to uncover the truth.

At the Swanson family home, a small yet powerful symbol of hope flickered in the darkness each night. They left their porch light on, an ever-burning beacon through the long, uncertain nights, symbolizing their undying hope that Brandon would one day return or be found. This nightly ritual, a silent vigil, continued steadfastly.

As the seasons turned and the landscape changed, the search efforts for Brandon resumed with renewed vigor. In the late fall, after the fields that had been sown shortly after Brandon's disappearance were harvested, search teams, accompanied by dogs trained to detect human remains, revisited the area. These canine units led searchers into a previously unexplored area northwest of Porter, following scents that hinted at human presence.

With the arrival of spring, as the snow melted away but before the fields were again claimed by planting, search efforts intensified once more. This cycle of searching, dictated by the rhythms of nature and agriculture, continued through to 2011. By this time, an astonishing expanse of 122 square miles had been meticulously combed through in the quest to find Brandon.

In a significant development in 2010, the case took on a new dimension as the Minnesota Bureau of Criminal Apprehension assumed the role of lead agency. With fresh resources and perspectives, the Bureau set up a dedicated tip line, a conduit for the public to contribute any information they might have. By the year 2015, this initiative had garnered 90 leads, a testament to the case's enduring impact and the community's commitment to finding answers.

As official searches resumed, the focus of the investigation shifted towards Mud Creek, a tributary of the Yellow Medicine River, located north and northwest of Porter. This new area of interest opened up yet another chapter in the ongoing saga of Brandon Swanson's disappearance, a mystery that continued to captivate and haunt all those who hoped for a resolution.

Among the most poignant aspects of this mystery were the diverging beliefs and theories held by those closest to the case. Annette Swanson, Brandon's mother, found herself grappling with the unsettling possibilities suggested by the search dogs' actions. One of the dogs had tracked a scent to the Yellow Medicine River, but intriguingly, its trail didn't end there. Instead, the dog continued its pursuit across the river, up the opposite bank, and along another gravel road stretching north towards the Yellow Medicine County line. This trail, vanishing into the unknown, led Annette to believe that the river did not hold the answer to her son's fate. In her heart, she felt that there was no concrete indication that Brandon had met his end in the river's depths.

Brian Swanson, reflecting on his last interactions with his son, also harbored doubts about the likelihood of an accident. Despite any effects of alcohol Brandon might have experienced earlier in the evening, his demeanor during their phone conversations didn't suggest disorientation or confusion, adding another layer of complexity to the puzzle.

The question of whether Brandon might still be alive opened up a myriad of other remote possibilities. One such scenario was that he might have intentionally chosen to disappear, a notion that his parents struggled to accept, knowing their son. Sheriff Vizecky, keeping an open mind, couldn't entirely dismiss the possibility of foul play. However, with no tangible evidence to support this theory, it remained a speculative shadow in the backdrop of the investigation.

As the search for Brandon continued, the Swansons' experience sparked a broader conversation about the response to missing adult cases. Annette was particularly struck by the initial reaction of the Lynd police, who suggested that Brandon had the right to be missing due to his age. "I'm his mother and I knew something was horribly wrong," she later reflected on her instincts that tragic night. Motivated by their ordeal, Annette and Brian began advocating for legislative changes in Minnesota. Their goal was to ensure that missing adult cases received the same immediate attention and urgency as those involving possibly abducted children.

Their advocacy led Annette to meet with Marty Seifert, then the minority leader of the state House of Representatives. In a local restaurant, they discussed the challenges she faced with the police when reporting Brandon missing. Seifert, moved by Annette's determination to make a difference for others, even if it was too late for her son, introduced a bill that would come to be known as "Brandon's Law." This bill sought to amend the state's existing Missing Child Program, changing the word "child" to "person," thereby broadening its scope to include adults.

The journey of "Brandon's Law" through the legislative process was not without its challenges. Seifert recalled encountering initial resistance from the law enforcement community, particularly concerning privacy issues related to emerging technologies like cell phone tracking. These discussions revolved around the delicate balance between the urgency of finding missing persons and respecting privacy rights, a conversation emblematic of the evolving digital age.

Brandy Hanna

B randy Renee, born on the 16th of November, 1972, entered the world as the cherished first child and only daughter of Donna Hanna, later known as Donna Parent. From the moment of her birth, Brandy was the apple of her mother's eye, enveloped in a deep and abiding love. Raised in a nurturing and supportive environment, Brandy's early years were enriched by the presence of extended family members, including aunts and uncles, who played a significant role in her upbringing. This strong family network, combined with Donna's unwavering affection, created a warm and loving world for Brandy, one that would later expand with the arrival of her younger brothers, Shane and Michael.

Brandy, with her striking blond hair and captivating blue eyes, was a natural charmer from a young age. Despite her inherent shyness, she possessed a magnetic charisma that effortlessly drew people towards her. This unique blend of timidity and allure was not lost on her friend Robin Pyle, who later reminisced, "Brandy had this incredible ability to transform the mundane into something extraordinarily fun and exciting. She was immensely creative." This creativity wasn't just a fleeting aspect of her personality; it was a driving force behind her artistic talents. Whenever she had a spare moment and a pencil in hand, Brandy could be found deeply immersed in her world of drawing and sketching.

Growing up, Brandy was often described as a tomboy, reveling in the joys of outdoor play, getting dirty, and simply having fun. Her athleticism and strength were as evident as her gentle, sensitive side. She was a unique blend of humor and eclecticism, paired with a caring, sweet, and loving nature – qualities that reflected the family environment she had grown up in.

During her high school years, Brandy's adventurous spirit and love for physical activities led her to join the Reserve Officers' Training Corps (ROTC), an experience that further shaped her character. Throughout these formative years, her bond with her mother Donna continued to deepen, evolving into a relationship that many would liken to that of best friends. Donna, taking her role as a mother to heart, found herself constantly charmed by Brandy, as did most people who had the fortune of crossing paths with her. Their relationship was one of mutual reliance; Brandy saw her mother as her rock, a constant in her life she could always depend on, and for Donna, Brandy was a source of immense joy and pride.

Brandy's life was predominantly centered around North Charleston, South Carolina. This vibrant city, known for its cultural diversity and contrasting neighborhoods, exposed Brandy to a myriad of experiences and people. As she navigated through her teenage years, Brandy, like many adolescents, started feeling the pressure to dress fashionably and make more expensive purchases. Sensing an opportunity for Brandy to earn her own money, Donna suggested she take up a job as a waitress. Initially hesitant due to her shyness, Brandy eventually found work at a local restaurant named Pappy, located in the town of Hanahan. This job marked the beginning of a transformative journey for Brandy; her continuous interaction with customers gradually chipped away at her shyness, revealing more of her vibrant personality and charm. This newfound confidence did not go unnoticed – customers began requesting her by name, drawn to the magnetic charisma that once again shone through.

This path ultimately led Brandy to decide to follow in her mother's footsteps and pursue a career in the restaurant industry. She thrived in this bustling environment, enjoying the company of her colleagues and the constant stream of customers. Her decision was further solidified when, in her mid-20s, she fell in love with Michael Rea McAdams Jr., known to most as Rhea. Their relationship blossomed rapidly, filling Brandy's life with happiness and love. Amy, Rhea's sister-in-law, would soon become one of Brandy's closest friends, further intertwining her life with Rhea's family.

However, life has a way of presenting unforeseen challenges. In late 1999, when Brandy and Rhea's relationship was nearly six years in, it was unexpectedly tested. Rhea's close friend, Garland Lankford, known as Zeke, found himself in a difficult situation following a separation from his wife. In a gesture of friendship, Rhea offered Zeke a place to stay. Little did they know, this act of kindness would set off a series of events that would forever alter their lives. An unexpected and initially resisted attraction developed between Brandy and Zeke. Despite their efforts to suppress these feelings, they grew stronger, leading to a complex and emotionally charged situation.

In March 2005, Brandy, now 32, took a new job as a waitress at Alex's Restaurant, where her mother had been working for over 30 years and was now a manager. This new job brought Brandy and her mother even closer, as they looked forward to spending more

time together. However, just a month later, the truth about Brandy and Zeke's feelings came to light, either through Brandy's confession or Rhea's discovery. Heartbroken, Rhea asked Zeke to leave and confronted Brandy with a choice: stay and work on their relationship or leave with Zeke. Despite Rhea's love and the comfort of their shared home, Brandy chose to follow her heart and start a new life with Zeke.

This decision led Brandy and Zeke to search for an apartment, preferably near Alex's Restaurant, as Brandy didn't own a car. Their financial constraints limited their options, and they eventually settled in Shakoora Cherokee, a neighborhood with a somewhat dubious reputation. This choice concerned Donna, who later expressed her apprehensions about her daughter living in an area known for crime and drugs.

Brandy's journey, marked by love, challenges, and choices, is a testament to her resilience and the unwavering support of her family. Her life, a tapestry of experiences ranging from her artistic pursuits to her adventures in the restaurant industry, paints a vivid picture of a woman who, despite facing adversity, remained true to herself and her heart.

Donna Parent, despite her reservations, found herself in a difficult position when her daughter, Brandy, and Brandy's partner, Zeke, approached her for a loan to cover the security deposit for their new apartment. The apartment, while nice and conveniently located just 1.3 miles from Alex's Restaurant on Florida Avenue, was situated in an area that Donna deemed unsuitable for her daughter. However, Zeke's insistence on this particular location and Brandy's excitement about moving in together overrode Donna's concerns. Reluctantly, Donna agreed to the loan, albeit with a sense of frustration, feeling that her efforts to guide Brandy to a better location were being undermined by Zeke's influence.

Once settled into their new home, Brandy's brother Shane observed a noticeable uplift in her spirits, remarking that she seemed genuinely content with her new living situation. Brandy was committed to making the best of it, balancing her job at Alex's Restaurant and her relationship with Zeke. However, the dynamic was complicated by Zeke's ongoing divorce and the emotional toll it was taking on him. Adding to the complexity, Brandy's ex, Ray, was persistent in his attempts to reconcile, often visiting her at work to plead his case.

A particularly unsettling incident occurred during one of Ray's visits to the restaurant. In a conversation with Donna, Ray made a disturbing comment, suggesting he could harm Brandy without consequence. Donna, shocked by the remark, initially dismissed it as an attempt by Ray to assert some form of control or dominance, especially in her presence. This interaction, however, planted seeds of unease that would later resurface in Donna's mind.

Brandy's life took another dramatic turn when, unexpectedly, Zeke announced his decision to return to his wife and children. His abrupt departure left Brandy heartbroken and alone in the apartment they had shared. Despite her deep feelings for Zeke, Brandy respected his choice to return to his family, not wanting to be the reason for the breakdown of a marriage.

In the wake of this emotional upheaval, Brandy chose to remain in the apartment, using this time to reflect and heal from her recent heartbreaks. Her friend Robyn noted that Brandy held onto a sliver of hope that Zeke might return, suspecting his departure was more a result of cold feet than a final decision.

As word of the breakup spread, Ray intensified his efforts to win Brandy back. During this time, Brandy confided in Robyn about her fear of Ray, although she did not elaborate on the specifics of her apprehensions. This fear wasn't entirely surprising to those who knew them; Ray's presence often cast a disconcerting aura, marked by what some perceived as a controlling nature or an intimidating demeanor.

On May 19th, 2005, Brandy met with Ray's sister-in-law, Amy McAdams, at Pappy's Restaurant. The two enjoyed their time together, with Brandy expressing her desire to take a beach trip that weekend. Amy agreed to accompany Brandy shopping for a new bathing suit the following evening. This would be their last meeting.

On May 20th, Brandy worked her usual shift at Alex's, seeming upbeat and hopeful about possibly reconnecting with Zeke. However, a phone call during her shift visibly shook her, concerning both her coworkers and regular customers. The call, related to Zeke's wife Diana, left Brandy unsettled but she soon regained her composure.

That evening, despite making plans with Amy for shopping, Brandy never responded to knocks at her apartment door. Amy, assuming Brandy had fallen asleep, left without further investigation.

Over the next few days, Donna's attempts to contact Brandy went unanswered, heightening her anxiety. She speculated that Brandy might be at the beach, but the unusual lack of communication was troubling. Donna's concern escalated when Brandy failed to show up for her scheduled shift on May 23rd.

As hours turned into days without any word from Brandy, her family and friends grew increasingly alarmed. Brandy's typical routine involved regular contact with her loved ones, particularly on Sundays when they gathered for breakfast. The absence of her presence and the silence of her phone painted a worrying picture. Donna, grappling with her instincts and the eerie premonition she had felt days earlier, feared that something was amiss.

Donna Parent's brief moment of relief, under the assumption that Brandy had shown up for her shift at the restaurant, was shattered by a phone call around 7:20 AM. An employee informed her that Brandy had not arrived for work, a highly unusual occurrence given Brandy's dedication and love for her job. This was the first glaring sign that something was amiss. The stark deviation from Brandy's habitual punctuality and responsibility set off alarm bells for Donna, leading her to believe that her daughter was in trouble.

With a growing sense of urgency, Donna contacted the North Charleston Police Department to file a missing person report. However, the response she received was disheartening; the police treated the situation with a degree of indifference typical for cases involving adults who may have chosen to leave of their own volition. They explained to Donna that if they launched an investigation for every adult who disappeared without notice, they would be overwhelmed and unable to address other crimes. Despite Donna's insistence that something was wrong, the authorities initially perceived the situation as a case of a worried mother unable to reach her daughter.

Desperate for any lead, Donna reached out to Zeke. She knew he still had a key to the apartment and requested his assistance in gaining access to check if Brandy was there. Zeke, who was on a plumbing job at the time, agreed to meet Donna at the apartment. Donna had specifically asked Zeke to wait for her before entering the apartment, but upon her arrival, she was dismayed to find him exiting the building. Confronting Zeke about why he had disregarded her request, she was taken aback by his response. He mentioned his fear that Donna might find Brandy's body inside, a statement that left Donna both shocked and confused.

Entering the apartment, Donna found everything in order, with no signs of a struggle or forced entry. The to-go cup of tea Brandy had filled on Friday was still there, along with a blanket on the couch, indicating that Brandy had likely been relaxing as she typically did. Her prepaid phone was on the nightstand, charging, but the phone Donna had recently bought her was missing. The only other items absent were the apartment keys, suggesting that Brandy had left with the intention of returning but never did.

As the days passed with no word from Brandy, Donna's anxiety escalated. Four days later, on May 27th, one week after Brandy was last seen, the North Charleston Police Department finally agreed to initiate an investigation. However, precious time had already been lost – a critical factor in missing person cases.

A detective assigned to the case conducted a brief examination of the apartment but found nothing amiss and no evidence of a crime, which only added to Donna's frustration. Feeling that the police were not taking Brandy's disappearance seriously enough, she mobilized friends and family to search for her daughter.

Given Brandy's distinct appearance – a blue-eyed, blonde-haired young woman – in a predominantly African-American neighborhood, the family hoped she would be easily remembered. They went door-to-door, inquiring about any sightings of Brandy, but most neighbors only recalled seeing her in the past, walking to or from work.

In their efforts to find Brandy, missing person flyers were distributed through-out the neighborhood. The flyers featured Brandy's image, description, and last-known location, in hopes that someone might come forward with information.

Brandy's connections to law enforcement through her Uncle Henry Smalley Jr., a member of the North Charleston Police Department, and family friend Lieutenant Rick Keyes, who was not officially assigned to the case, provided additional resources in the search. Smalley expressed concern about an old abandoned Naval Base nearby, a sprawling complex known for illicit activities and as a potential place to conceal a body. Along with friends and family, Smalley thoroughly searched the base, but no evidence of Brandy's presence was found.

During the canvassing near Brandy's apartment, Lieutenant Keyes spoke with a neighbor, Jevetta Johnson, who claimed not only to have seen Brandy but also to have witnessed her on the night she disappeared. This revelation offered a glimmer of hope in the search for Brandy, as it could potentially lead to new information about her whereabouts on that fateful night. The family's determination to uncover the truth about Brandy's disappearance drove them to continue their relentless search, clinging to any shred of hope that might lead them to find her.

Jevetta Johnson's eyewitness account provided investigators with a crucial piece of information about Brandy Hanna's disappearance. Between 9:00 and 9:30 p.m. on that fateful Friday, Johnson observed a truck pulling into the parking lot. She witnessed Brandy exiting her apartment and getting into the passenger seat, engaging in a conversation with the driver. Although Johnson did not see the truck leave and didn't watch for an extended period, she managed to get a clear view of both the truck and its driver. The driver was described as a white male with scraggly hair and a beard, driving a distinctive red truck with a white stripe and a Jason Voorhees-style hockey mask affixed to the front grille.

This description was particularly significant as it matched two individuals in Brandy's life: Ray McAdams and Zeke Lankford. Both were Caucasian men with similar physical characteristics and drove red trucks. However, the unique detail of the hockey mask pointed specifically towards Ray's vehicle.

Lieutenant Rick Keyes, looking to confirm Johnson's account, planned a strategic identification. He drove Johnson to Ray McAdams' residence, maintaining communication with her via a Bluetooth earpiece as he approached the door. Upon seeing Ray, Johnson immediately and emphatically identified him as the man she had seen driving the truck on the night Brandy disappeared. Her certainty was undeniable, as Keyes noted her excitement and confidence in the identification.

With these developments, the investigation began to narrow down its focus on two primary suspects: Ray McAdams and Zeke Lankford. Both men were interrogated about their whereabouts on the night of May 20th. Ray provided an alibi, claiming he was at a club applying for a bouncer position until the early hours of the morning, corroborated by a friend. Zeke, on the other hand, stated he had intended to visit Brandy but got held up with work, a claim confirmed by his brother-in-law.

Each man suggested the other as a possible suspect in Brandy's disappearance. Zeke expressed his fear of the worst, given Brandy's troubled history with her ex-boyfriend Ray. The investigators found themselves at a deadlock, with both suspects providing alibis and implicating each other.

The police began tailing Ray and Zeke, delving deeper into their backgrounds. Ray agreed to a polygraph test a week later, which he reportedly passed. Zeke also consented to the test but delayed it for nearly two months. When he finally took it, despite his nervous demeanor, he passed as well.

With no concrete evidence linking either man to Brandy on the night she vanished, the investigators were back at square one. Even Johnson's identification of Ray, while intensifying the focus on him, wasn't enough to solidify a case.

The media attention on May 30th, ten days after Brandy's disappearance, was overwhelmingly focused on Natalie Holloway, an 18-year-old who vanished in Aruba. This coverage overshadowed Brandy's case, much to Donna's dismay and frustration. It was a bitter pill for Donna, who struggled to understand why her daughter's disappearance was not receiving similar media attention. Her efforts to bring Brandy's case into the spotlight finally bore fruit when The Post and Courier responded to her pleas, publishing the first of several articles about Brandy's disappearance.

In a turn of events that could potentially impact the investigation, Brandy's landlord contacted Donna. The lease was only paid up until the end of the month, and Donna was faced with the decision to either remove Brandy's belongings or have them discarded. With the apartment not classified as a crime scene, Donna and her sister Yvonne were left to clear out Brandy's possessions. During this process, they discovered a can of cash from Brandy's tips and paychecks and noticed that none of her clothing or a cherished baby photo of Brandy in Donna's arms was missing. This discovery further dispelled any notion that Brandy might have left of her own accord.

However, this cleanup meant that any potential forensic evidence in the apartment was lost. The case, now gaining some attention, continued to hit dead ends. Tips and leads went nowhere, and local informants had no information on Brandy's whereabouts.

As the investigation lingered with little progress, the case was gradually growing cold. The lack of tangible evidence and viable leads left the authorities with scant resources to pursue. In an attempt to reinvigorate the search and possibly uncover new information, the CUE (Community United Effort) Center for Missing Persons became involved in August, about three months after Brandy's disappearance. Their first official search employed tracking dogs and items infused with Brandy's scent, hoping to trace her path on the night she vanished. The North Charleston Police Department joined this effort, along with a multitude of volunteers, including Brandy's friends, family, and concerned locals.

One individual present at the search, however, raised eyebrows. Zeke Lankford, a person of interest in the case, was observed attentively monitoring the search efforts. His presence became a point of concern, particularly when he approached Donna's niece and inquired about the tracking dogs' ability to locate Brandy if she were buried. This unnerving question prompted investigators to advise Zeke against attending future searches and to keep his distance from Brandy's family.

In parallel, a large banner featuring Brandy's missing person flyer was displayed prominently outside Alex's Restaurant. This banner, visible to passersby on the nearby interstate, was intended to generate more public awareness and hopefully elicit additional tips. Unfortunately, the search and the banner did not lead to any significant breakthroughs.

Several months later, in April 2006, 11 months after Brandy's disappearance, Donna received distressing news. Ray McAdams' mother informed her of Ray's sudden death due to a heart attack. If Ray had any knowledge about what happened to Brandy, that information was now irretrievably lost. Donna had been torn between suspecting Ray's involvement and considering the possibility of his innocence. Despite Ray's cooperative demeanor with authorities and his participation in searches and vigils, inconsistencies in his story had raised doubts.

Further complicating the situation, Amy, Brandy's friend and Ray's sister-in-law, revealed that she had dropped items off to Ray around 9:30 p.m. on the night of Brandy's disappearance, contradicting Ray's alibi of being at a club.

This revelation, however, could not be pursued further due to Ray's passing.

Tragically, just two weeks after Ray's death, Brandy's Uncle Henry Smalley Jr., a dedicated member of the search effort, succumbed to cancer. Among his final promises to Donna was a vow to seek answers about Brandy's fate in the afterlife.

Over the years, numerous tips and leads emerged, but none led to any concrete information about Brandy's whereabouts. One disturbing incident involved a man impersonating a police officer approaching Donna, who was later arrested for his impersonation. Brandy's family continued to honor her memory, holding annual birthday celebrations and candlelight vigils.

In 2010, five years after Brandy's disappearance, Donna expressed her enduring pain and determination to find answers. Her relentless pursuit of the truth led her to consult a psychic in West Virginia for any possible insight.

In February 2011, Sergeant Ron Locker of the North Charleston Police Department took a personal interest in the case after repeatedly noticing the missing-persons banner at Alex's Restaurant. With Donna's permission, he decided to reopen the investigation, meticulously reviewing the existing case files and re-interviewing initial witnesses.

Locker was disheartened to find that many potential leads had not been thoroughly investigated. Key aspects, such as the phone call Brandy received at work the day she vanished, had not been tracked, and phone records were no longer available. Furthermore, no forensic testing had been conducted on the trucks belonging to Ray McAdams or Zeke Lankford's father's plumbing business.

Reexamining witness Jevetta Johnson's testimony, Locker found her account consistent over the years. However, when presented with a photo lineup,

Johnson identified Zeke Lankford, not Ray McAdams, as the driver she saw on the night Brandy disappeared. This discrepancy raised questions about the reliability of her initial identification.

Locker shifted his focus to determine what might have happened to Brandy and where she could be. He theorized that she might have been a victim of homicide and began searching areas near her former apartment for potential burial sites. His attention was drawn to the old abandoned naval base, an area that had undergone significant changes since 2005. With parts of the land turned into a waterfront park, the terrain offered numerous potential hiding spots for a body.

In his personal time, Locker dedicated himself to searching these areas, hoping to uncover any clue that might lead to Brandy. His commitment to finding answers reflected the ongoing anguish and unanswered questions surrounding Brandy Hanna's mysterious disappearance.

One evening, Sergeant Ron Locker's investigative efforts led him to a peculiar site under what was once a pier. Compelled by an inexplicable intuition, he waited for the low tide to access the sand and mud hidden beneath. As he dug near a concrete wall, his shovel struck an object buried in the ground. Unearthing it revealed a circular ring, the kind used to seal 55-gallon drums, and more intriguingly, a shoe. It was a woman's blue and white Nike cross-trainer, size ten and a half. On the last day she was seen, Brandy was reported to be wearing a similar pair of newly purchased blue and white Nike cross trainers. Although Brandy wore a size 10, it's not uncommon for individuals to buy cross trainers a half size to a full size larger. The shoe's manufacturing date, marked January 25, 2005, was just four months before Brandy disappeared.

Locker immediately sent the shoe for DNA analysis and called in the state's archaeologists to conduct a thorough search of the area for any additional clues, such as bone fragments or clothing. Despite their exhaustive efforts over three days, no further evidence was found, and the DNA analysis of the shoe came back inconclusive. But for Locker, the circumstantial evidence was compelling. The shoe's size, color, make, and manufacturing date, coupled with its location in a remote area, led him to strongly believe that it belonged to Brandy.

Locker theorized that Brandy's body might have been initially buried in the golf course area and later drifted into the Cooper River due to the encroaching salt marsh. The currents could have carried her remains further, potentially leaving the shoe where he found it. He remained convinced that somewhere in that vicinity lay the remains of Brandy Hanna.

The case was a challenging one for Locker. With no substantial evidence or definitive clues, and only opinions and hearsay regarding potential suspects, it was an uphill battle. However, significant developments would soon unfold.

In 2012, Alex's Restaurant, a pivotal location in Brandy's life, closed its doors, marking the end of an era. The following year, Brandy was legally declared dead. Then, in December 2016, a significant break occurred in the case. Garland "Zeke" Lankford, already incarcerated in Berkeley County Jail for first-degree criminal sexual misconduct, was arrested in connection with Brandy's disappearance. This development was spurred by a tipster who alleged knowledge of Lankford and two others' potential involvement.

During interviews with Locker, inconsistencies emerged in Lankford's original statements. Despite claiming to have worked late on the night of Brandy's disappearance, business records showed he clocked out at 4:00 p.m. Additionally, Lankford had initially stated that Ray McAdams had been contacting him about Brandy, but phone records contradicted this, showing Lankford as the initiator. When confronted, Lankford admitted to seeing Brandy on the night she vanished and to making false tip calls to investigators.

Faced with the evidence of his deception, Lankford was charged with obstruction of justice. To avoid a potential 10-year prison sentence, he pleaded guilty and received a two-year sentence followed by two years of probation.

In a surprising twist, Ray McAdams' father, Michael, approached Sergeant Locker with a story he had heard. According to Michael, Lankford had been entangled with drug dealers and used Brandy as collateral to settle his debts, leading to her being taken away. While the veracity of this story remained uncertain, it added another layer of complexity to the already intricate case.

In the perplexing case of Brandy Hanna's disappearance, recent developments have steered Sergeant Ron Locker's investigation towards a specific set of theories. Locker's determination and the tireless efforts of Donna Parent, Brandy's mother, have narrowed down the possibilities to two main theories, dismissing the likelihood that Brandy left voluntarily, was abducted by a stranger, or fell victim to a random act of violence.

The first theory posits Ray McAdams' potential involvement in Brandy's disappearance, either acting alone or in collaboration with Garland "Zeke" Lankford. For many involved in the case, a multitude of details seem to implicate both men, raising suspicions that it wasn't the act of just one individual.

The second theory focuses on Zeke Lankford, hypothesizing that he, along with two associates, visited Brandy's apartment under the pretense of discussing their relationship. This theory suggests that the encounter took a fatal turn, leading to Brandy's murder and the disposal of her body near the Cooper River in North Charleston. The specifics of whether this was a premeditated act or a tragic outcome of an altercation remain unclear. However, this theory accuses Lankford of causing Brandy's death, attempting to derail the investigation, and directing suspicion towards McAdams. Some even speculate that Lankford may have trafficked Brandy to settle a drug debt.

Brandy Renee Hanna was last seen as a Caucasian female with blond hair and blue eyes, standing five feet nine inches tall, and weighing approximately 115 pounds. She was wearing a light blue shirt, jeans, and blue and white Nike shoes, along with a distinct diamond ring. Her physical characteristics included crooked upper teeth with a gap between the front ones, pierced ears, and two tattoos – a heart between her right thumb and forefinger and a sun on her right shoulder. Her blood type is A positive.

Despite the ongoing investigation, much of the early evidence was flawed or insufficient, leaving the suspects, though under suspicion, not conclusively linked to Brandy's disappearance. Lankford's conviction for obstruction of justice has not bridged the gap to a charge of homicide.

For Donna Parent, the years since her daughter's disappearance have been fraught with pain and uncertainty. She holds onto the belief that Brandy was murdered and clings to the hope that the full truth will eventually surface. Her desire is not only for justice but also for the chance to lay her daughter to rest properly, to have a place to mourn and say a final goodbye.

The recent progress in the investigation, particularly with new leads and the involvement of dedicated officers like Sergeant Locker, offers a glimmer of hope. The investigators remain optimistic, believing that with additional information or a breakthrough tip, they will be able to solve the long-standing mystery of Brandy Hanna's disappearance.

Bibliography

Associated Press. "Police charge former boyfriend in woman's 2005 disappearance." The Post and Courier, 28 Dec. 2022.

Barndt, Christine. "Keeping the Faith: A Family's Search." Missing Kids, 7 July 2020.

Bauer, Tedd. "What happened to Jeramy Carl Burt?" Medium, 7 Feb. 2022.

Baxter, Jenn. "Abducted While Using a Payphone: What Happened to Angela Hammond?" Medium, 16 July 2023.

Bell, Adam. "Gaston County Police still searching for woman missing since 2008." Charlotte Observer, 1 Apr. 2015.

Bryce, Debbie. "American Falls man missing since 2007: Mother believes he was the victim of foul play." Idaho State Journal, 28 Mar. 2014.

Charley Project. "Brandy Renee Hanna." The Charley Project, 22 Dec. 2016.

Charley Project. "Diamond Yvette Bradley." The Charley Project, 23 Sept. 2021.

Charley Project, Project. "Brandi Ellen Wells." The Charley Project, 15 May 2019.

Charley Project, Project. "Kayla May Bert." The Charley Project, 12 Oct. 2004.

Charley Project, The. "Logan Schiendelman." The Charley Project, 27 Sept. 2018.

Comme, Pamela. "20 years since the disappearance of Rachel Cooke, family remains hopeful." KVUE, 9 Jan. 2022.

Denton, Gloria. "A Mother Unearths Vital Evidence Investigators Missed." Missing Piece, 5 Dec. 2006.

Dickson, Amelia. "When Thurston County residents disappear without a trace." The Olympian, 14 Jan. 2017.

Disappeared. "Brandy Hanna." Disappeared Blog, 11 Dec. 2020.

Dowell, Liz. "Note offers clues in 'mistaken' 1991 Missouri abduction." Fox 2, 29 Jan 2023.

Duggan, Alexandra. "Two Boise men went missing three years apart. An intricate web of connections might link their cold cases." KTVB7, 24 Mar. 2022.

Farrow, Libbi. "Rachel Cooke still missing more than 20 years later." Fox 7 Houston, 3 Dec. 2023.

Hallmark, Bob. "Fourth Search For Brandi Wells." KLTV, 4 Aug. 2007.

Hemraj, Fatim. "After a Teen Disappeared, a 'Friend' Told Her Parents a Disturbing Story." Vocal Media, May 2023.

Hirsch, Deborah. "Man in trunk 'of interest' in open case." The Charlotte Observer, 10 June 2008.

Howard, Wayne. "Gaston Police Renew Search For Jamie Fraley." Lincoln Herald, 1 Apr. 2015.

Jackson, David. "Tionda & Diamond Bradley." Chicago Tribune, 20 July 2013.

Kevlin, T.A. Headless Man in Topless Bar: Studies of 725 cases of strip club related criminal homicides. 25 Apr. 2007.

Kruger, Rae. "Search for teen continues." Marshall Independent, 16 May 2008.

Liu, Erin. "Nine years later, Kayla Berg still missing." WSAW, 11 Aug. 2018.

Link, Bob. "Court declares Jodi Huisentruit legally dead." Globe Gazette, 15 May 2001.

Manoukian, Marina. "The Tragic Story Of The Clinton Avenue 5." Grunge.com, 4 Apr. 2022.

Mastre, Brian. "Cold Case: News Anchor Abducted." WOWT, 10 July 2015.

Mattera, Jason. "Where is Logan Schiendelman? Young man vanishes from Olympia area." True Crime Daily, 16 May 2017.

Mysteries, Unsolved. "Desperately Seeking Susan." Unsolved Mysteries, 26 Jan. 2021.

Pasqualini, Kim. "Where Is Rachel Cooke?" The Crime Wire, 10 Oct. 2023.

Pieper, Mary. "Search for Jodi Huisentruit continues 20 years later." Globe Gazette, 27 June 2015.

Porter, David. "Nation & World | Murder charges filed in case of 5 missing NJ teens." Seattle Times Newspaper.

Rietmulder, Michael. "The search for Brandon Swanson continues seven years later." City Pages, 16 Oct. 2015.

S, Sophia. "The Mysterious Disappearance of April Pitzer." Medium, 5 Oct. 2022.

Scott, Robert. Suddenly She Was Gone. Rivers of Blood. New York: Pinnacle, 2009.

Sullivan, Alfred. "Susan Walsh Story." Alfredsullivan.com, 1998.

Tresnowski, Alex. "Into Thin Air." People, 23 Mar. 1998.

Tuttle, Greg. "Sheriff believes Amy Wroe Bechtel was victim of killer." Billings Gazette, 21 June 2007.

Unfound. "Brandi Wells: What The Camera Saw." Unfound Podcast, 28 Apr. 2017.

Weed, Alexis. "Teen drove into ditch, vanished as parents searched." CNN, 18 Jan. 2010.

9 7 9 8 8 6 9 1 8 0 6 6 7